Finlay J. Macdonald, known to thousands of BBC radio listeners for his delightful 'Crowdie and Cream' talks, can look back on a long and successful career as a radio drama and talks producer, and then as a television director. For the TV documentary 'A Drop in the Ocean' his script and researches in the Hebridean island of Uist investigated the facts behind Compton McKenzie's *Whisky Galore*, and his *Journey to the Western Isles* retraces the steps of Johnson and Boswell 200 years ago. He lives near Glasgow, working as a writer, editor and broadcaster.

Also by Finlay J. Macdonald

CROWDIE AND CREAM

FINLAY J. MACDONALD

Crotal and White

Futura

To Les Robinson,
who started it all

A Futura Book

© Finlay J. Macdonald 1983

First published in Great Britain in 1983 by
Macdonald & Co (Publishers) Ltd
London & Sydney

First Futura edition 1984

ISBN 0 7088 2576 1

Reproduced, printed and bound in Great Britain by
Hazell Watson & Viney Limited,
Member of the BPCC Group,
Aylesbury, Bucks

Futura Publications
A Division of
Macdonald & Co (Publishers) Ltd
Maxwell House
74 Worship Street
London EC2A 2EN
A BPCC plc Company

Chapter One

I have very few certificates to prove that I ever achieved anything, and the lack of them may be, in itself, certification of the real truth! But I have one which I treasure, although I have no recollection of ever deserving or winning it. It is headed *CHURCH OF SCOTLAND Sunday School* and goes on to say *Awarded to Finlay Macdonald for Regular Attendance and Good Conduct. (Signed) Adèle Kerr. Manse. Scarista.* Like that famous portrait of Dorian Gray the certificate has retained its pristine freshness while the years have etched their lines on the face and soul and conscience of its possessor! I remember well the night on which it should have been presented to me, and why it wasn't. . . .

Today the great big manse to which it refers still stands like a Manor House overlooking what remains of the village that my father and seven other ex-servicemen of the First World War carved out of South Harris half a century ago. It was built two hundred and fifty years ago when a huge population were in thrall to landlords of doubtful social morality, men who held the land as if by divine right and as a means of creating wealth for themselves and their descendants. The 'people' were the tools for the extraction of the wealth and, in the nineteenth century in particular, those people lived in conditions which were described by one traveller as being 'in many ways inferior to those of the American negro slaves'. Certainly they were colder, because the main source of landlord wealth in the early 1800s was the collection of seaweed, or kelp, for drying and burning into a powder which was a rich and valuable source of soda and iodine and many other by-products. The landlords made fortunes, which many of them squandered on high living in London and other European capitals; the workers were paid pennies and lived in crowded squalor on the Atlantic shores. It is an old story, of which the memory may have lingered on too long.

In those days the minister was paid by the landlord and supplied with a palatial manse, which accommodated not only his own large family but also provided 'overflow' lodgings for the landlord's occasional summer guests. Inevitably, in time, the minister tended to become the laird's man rather than the Lord's man and put his own and his patron's worldly well-being before the needs of his flock. When the kelp industry collapsed and failed in the face of competition from imported chemicals the population of the Western Highlands became unemployed and unemployable and unwanted. Many of them starved. Thousands were shipped overseas in a pogrom which was, of its time, as ruthless as the Nazi solution of the Jewish 'problem'. The first huge batch of people evicted from the Southlands of Harris disappeared without trace. Their ship may have sunk, along with many others, somewhere in the Atlantic. Or it is just possible that they may have reached the maritime provinces of Canada. There were at least two more waves of eviction after that one, because the soft land of South Harris was highly desirable for successive generations of sheep farmers who did not require a large population to further their own selfish interests as the 'kelp lords' had done. Our huge manse and the church which stood beside it were monuments to those older times, but by the time our village was established we could barely muster a congregation of 30 in a church which had been built for four hundred.

The manse itself has long since been vacated in favour of a modern smaller building more suited to the modest aspirations and the greater continence of today's clergymen, but the old Georgian building still stands, surveying, as it has always done, some three thousand acres of the most beautiful country in Britain – lush meadowland, mountains that are forbidding or inviting according to the seasons and their moods, and an infinity of shell-white sand pounded by the combed breakers of an ocean whose other shore is Canada where live and prosper, perhaps, the descendants of that lost generation I spoke of.

They call it *Scarista House* now but it will always be 'the manse' to me. Its reputation grows year by year as a temple of good living, and on its altar, exotically disguised, are sacrificed the fishes and the molluscs which we regarded as the food of poverty but which, in a new age, attract the gourmet scribes who steal in anonymously to decide which of their gold and silver accolades they will bestow.

I have visited *Scarista House* only once in this new phase of its existence, and met for the first time the enterprising couple who have brought about its transformation. We talked of the old days that I remembered and the new future that they are creating. I was curious to know what memories of the past they had unearthed during their careful rehabilitation of the old building, what mementoes of those generations of successive pastors of varying personality and ability and divinity? A riding crop in the old stables, perhaps? A faded Victorian portrait in a cellar? A dusty tome in an attic?

'Nothing!' they said. With a curiosity as natural as my own they had scoured the old building from foundations to rafters expecting to find some clue to the character, good or bad, of one or other of their scores of predecessors, but it was as if God had decided to wipe the slate clean and leave no shred of evidence of the worldly frailties of his departed servants. Only the kitchen garden had yielded anything at all, and that was mystery rather than clue. When they had attempted to dig it over in order to add their own home-grown vegetables to their prestigious menus they found they couldn't sink a spade without a clink, as every upturned sod revealed a long-concealed bottle. Bottles upon bottles. And their lack of variety was monotonous in the extreme, even if puzzling in no small measure. The ones that hadn't once upon a time contained champagne, had contained that well known laxative known as *California Syrup of Figs*. Champagne and syrup of figs! An unlikely cocktail. Perhaps the old Scottish metrical psalm makes the only possible comment:

3

*The troubles that afflict the just
In numbers many be. . . .*

As I left the old manse and walked slowly down the path to
the new road – for which the foundations were being laid when
I was a boy in the new village – I smiled to myself at the
incongruity of champagne bottles hidden in the garden of a
Harris church house. Champagne! Of all things it was
probably the least known in our village. And then out of the
shadowy recesses of my memory came the name on my Sunday
School Certificate. Adèle! It certainly was not one of the
village's most common names. Involuntarily I glanced over
my shoulder back to the big house lest through a casement
window I might glimpse once more her friendly shade.

Mrs Kerr was the young widow of the old minister who had
died shortly after we had started making the village in the new
world of the Southlands. There is nothing unusual about an
old minister leaving a young widow, but what set Mrs Kerr
apart was that she was French. Or to be precise she was a
Channel Islander with a pedigree as French as Fifi; and how
she found herself in the remoteness of the Outer Hebrides as
a very young housekeeper to a Hebridean minister of advanced
middle age I shall never know. Legend has it that my Great
Aunt Rachel, who was employed in the manse at the time, saw
the minister and the housekeeper leave the manse one morning,
not to return till late evening. 'Rachel,' the minister is alleged
to have said when they got back, 'I should like you to call
Adèle "Mrs Kerr" from now on.' 'That,' said Aunt Rachel,
'is much more seemly.' And that was that.

Mrs Kerr must have been a very lonely woman in the years
of her widowhood. There was always a social barrier between
any incumbent of the manse and the local people, and it may
well have been exaggerated in our community by the fact that
our men were all ex-servicemen, some of whom had spent long
years in France during the First World War and, in their
occasionally expansive moments, were inclined to make sly
little references to nights on the town when they weren't in the
trenches. There was little about Mrs Kerr to suggest Mont-
martre or the Café de Paris, but, nevertheless, the village

4

women were inclined to look at her askance. Perhaps it was loneliness that made her, in a manner of speaking, *adopt* the school; and Miss Martin, our schoolmistress (ever receptive to anything that might help widen our horizons), was only too willing to give the lady from the manse the run of the classroom for the last couple of hours of some Friday afternoons. At that time I was just beginning to feel modestly confident in the very elementary stages of the English language, and it came as a shock when it was brought home to me by Mrs Kerr that there was a third language in the world, and maybe even more beyond!

It was Mrs Kerr also who introduced us to the festival of Christmas. Up till then Christmas had just been a date on the calendar, and our seasonal festivities had been confined to the two New Years – the newfangled one on the thirty-first day of December and the old one, celebrated by my Great Aunt Rachel's generation according to the Julian calendar on the twelfth of January. It was around the middle of November, if I remember rightly, that Mrs Kerr announced to us that Christmas was going to be on the twenty-fifth of December that year and that, to prove it, there was going to be a party in the manse.

The 13 of us who comprised the school glanced at each other uncomfortably and shuffled our winter boots on the floor – the nearest that the Hebridean school child of those days could ever get to enthusiasm or applause. Some discreet whispering reassured the more monoglot infants that 'a party was a good thing', and for the rest of the afternoon a general feeling of goodwill pervaded the green and yellow classroom. Only the teacher looked slightly flushed and apprehensive. Obviously the idea was new to her too and, in retrospect, as a member of the fundamentalist Free Presbyterian Church she must have had grave doubts about the propriety of celebrating a festival with slightly Papist overtones in the manse of a not-so-fundamentalist Church of Scotland. But Mrs Kerr was a magnanimous patron of the school in so many ways that a rejection of her plan would have been hurtful. In any case the teacher's reservations were slightly assuaged when Mrs Kerr added that the Sunday School Certificates would be handed out at the end of the proceedings; that must have seemed slightly like 'grace after meat' and from then on she entered into the scheme with enthusiasm.

At the end of the day we were each given a note to take home to our parents; notes which shattered the general bonhomie when they were read, as all such notes were read and assessed, at a conventicle convened below the red road-bridge on the way home. The notes stated baldly that a Christmas Treat would be held in the manse on the evening of 24 December and that all pupils would be kept in school for an extra hour each evening until then in order to prepare items for the party. One further cryptic sentence exhorted parents to assist children with any extra homework which might be involved. Homework! Big Hugh MacGregor, who would be leaving school come summer with barely enough education to be a carter, snorted and declared that if anybody farted in class the teacher would make it an excuse to give us a homework essay on flatulence. The boys laughed uproariously and the girls blushed, but the enthusiasm went out of us. Our only hope was that our parents might find some reason for objection – perhaps the one or two with the same severe attitudes to religion as the teacher – but it seemed a faint possibility; as far as most of the villagers were concerned, their respect for anything savouring of education was as profound as the teacher's own; part of her success was that she had so much of their backing. It was silently that we dropped off in our ones and twos at our respective gates.

At times of peat-cutting or of harvest our fathers and mothers might possibly have made some vague protest against the extra school hour on the grounds that it would be depriving them of extra hands to labour on the croft. But not in November.

November was a dead month in the village, and the nights were long. The brittle crispness of the autumn had vanished, and the school was already being disbanded at three o'clock because it was getting too dark to read. The winds were beginning to haunt the north and the west, and the gales would sometimes be salt from the sea. People didn't go out much at night, unless they had to, because, although we didn't know it, middle age – which came earlier then than now – was already creeping in on men who had married later than usual because they had lost the five most precious years of their lives in the war. The few, from the original population of the village, who were old enough for courting had nobody to court unless they went far afield, and – even if their loins were aching enough to tempt them face the blustery dark – experience had taught them that the soggy ground of winter made even the traditional nooks and crannies untempting for romance. And so all things conspired to cocoon people in their homes with their peat fires and their oil lamps. There was no radio as yet, and – unless a man was an avid reader like my father who would be beginning his annual foray into Gibbon's *Decline and Fall* . . . – they had little to do unless there was a tweed being prepared and the woman of the house needed help breaking up or 'teasing' the fleeces which she had dyed in the autumn, mixing the red-brown gobbets of coloured wool with tufts of untreated white in the exact proportions to give the shade of crotal and white which the water mill in the Northlands would blend and refine and return ready for spinning. That was the only part of the tweed-making process in which a man could help unless he was a weaver, which my father wasn't as yet. As boys, my brother and I could only be called on for occasional help because the mixing of the wool was crucial to the final blend.

As we approached the door I had little hope that either of our parents would raise any objection to the extra hour in school. On the contrary, I suspected that, like all the other parents of the village, they would welcome an extra hour of peace and quiet in the house, and greet any additional homework as something to keep us occupied during the winter nights. Mother had just lit the double-wick oil lamp as I got in and she was standing waiting for the glass funnel to warm before turning up the flame. I handed the teacher's note to father and he read it out aloud when the light went up.

'A Christmas Treat! Well, well, things are looking up for you young ones. Didn't I tell you some good would come out of going to Sunday School, and you grousing your heads off every Sunday afternoon. I wish somebody would organize a Christmas Treat for parents!'

My mother had been going to start setting the table for the evening meal once she'd got the lamp going to her satisfaction but she had stopped to listen.

'That'll be Mrs Kerr's idea,' she said. 'But she's forgetting something. How are you going to see what you're doing in school for an extra hour in the afternoon at this time of the year? You're already being allowed home early because of the dark.'

'Ach, you'd be surprised what French women can do in the dark.'

My mother slammed a dish on the table.

'And there'll be no shortage of fathers to go and meet the children when they get out!'

I noticed my father hiding a smile as he put his pipe in his mouth, but I didn't try to puzzle out what the interchange was about – as I usually did if I thought it was something I wasn't supposed to understand. All that concerned me was that my mother had almost certainly hit on something that Mrs Kerr and Miss Martin had overlooked, and that we might escape the extra hour of school after all. But the prospect wasn't totally pleasing. The idea of a party had been beginning to appeal to me – if a party was something like the wedding I'd been at, as, something suggested to me, it might well turn out to be.

We had all underestimated the resourcefulness of the two ladies in question. When Calum the Post came round with his red van on Saturday morning he knew all about the Christmas Treat.

'What a carry on,' I heard him saying to my father. 'I've got an order from the manse that will empty every shop in the Southlands of candles. She's the one who usually grumbles about the Royal Mail being used for free, but there's no word of that when she wants something herself. "Six dozen candles," says she. "And be sure you don't forget them!" The bloody schoolhouse is going to look like a lighthouse – if she doesn't set it on fire! Which wouldn't surprise me – her with her fancy French customs. Christmas in Paris is one thing; Christmas in Harris is something different altogether. It's bad enough the way things are going for me with all the extra mail that's beginning to flood in every year!'

8

Calum was still grumbling as he crunched the red van into gear. It wasn't like him. He happily carried bags of potatoes and sacks of raw tweed for the crofters without letting it worry his official conscience that not a penny was going into the coffers of the Post Office, but he hated being taken advantage of by anybody in the higher realms of society – as the inhabitants of the manse were deemed to be. However, even in those days, it was difficult to get out of the tentacles of the black economy once one succumbed to it, even for the most charitable of purposes, and Calum would doubtless come to terms with his qualms once he convinced himself, as he would, that he was really acting for the good of the children of the community. And once he remembered that the manse and the landlord's house were the only two establishments on his beat that crossed his palm with silver at Hogmanay instead of giving him a dram.

On Monday afternoon the candles were lit for the first time, as they were to be lit for each school afternoon for the forthcoming weeks. And we all conceded that they created a nice atmosphere in the classroom and gave it a character that was more pleasant than usual by far. As my mother had predicted, the fathers of the village didn't find it in the slightest burdensome to organize themselves into small posses to escort us home through the dark, although not for the reasons that she'd been hinting at. In a small country community the simplest little events became *occasions* when time otherwise tended to hang heavy, and for men without a pub, or any other social convenience to lighten the long hours, even meeting together at the schoolhouse for a brief yarn was a break from the darg.

Right through what remained of that long November and the December which followed we did an hour's overtime each school day and burnt up candles like a cathedral. And time and again, as new ideas came to the rejuvenated Mrs Kerr, hours of preparation were jettisoned and we set off on new tacks. The whole thing wasn't without its interests and excitements, for we were forever being introduced to concepts that were new to us. Carols, for example. Up till then our adventures into singing had been confined to the psalms of that David whom we had hitherto regarded as a poetical shepherd but who now turned out to have acquired a Royal City, and a few selected and highly improbable English songs from the prescribed text-book which had been subtly compiled to give us the impression that our own native culture and language had nothing of merit to offer us. Carols were something new altogether. They seemed to be trying to hide matters of mundanity in dresses of divinity and, for that very reason I suppose, Mrs Kerr and Miss Martin had to do some diplomatic horse-trading before they could agree on seasonal music that was acceptable to their divergent credos and mores. And there was also the matter of finding material that was suitable for the 12 ill-assorted voices of those who could sing – and me.

One that finally seemed to be mutually acceptable was *Good King Wenceslas*, presumably because he was an earthly king who didn't attempt to usurp the throne of the One higher up; because he was good; and because he had obvious leanings towards the new creed of socialism which was just beginning to filter across the Minch. At first I joined in the rehearsals with enthusiasm, which – when it came to singing – was always the last thing that anybody wanted from me, but the two ladies, on various pretexts, kept toning me down and down till at last I was reduced to a mere miming of the words and I lost interest. Instead, I passed the time for myself by attempting to unravel the meaning – if such there was – and the only way that I could get at the kernel of the meaning was by translating the whole thing laboriously into Gaelic for myself.

Good King Wenceslas looked out – that was simple and straightforward, even if there was no Gaelic for *Wenceslas*; the English did have some strange names after all. *On the feast of Stephen* was slightly more complicated, since the nearest approximation to a feast that I could envisage was Sunday dinner of salt mutton and potatoes or boiled chicken or rabbit . . . and splendid though they might be, those things didn't merit songs in our small part of the universe. But the whole thing lost its last claim to credibility on *When a poor man came in sight gathering winter fuel*. The nearest thing I knew to 'a poor man' was old Hector MacGeachan, who lived with his aged sister in a thatched black house on the moor's edge, and the only reason why I imagined him to be poor was because I'd heard people referring to him as 'poor old Hector', which I had thought was because he lived in a black house and not in a corrugated iron house like ours or one of the smart white stone and lime croft houses to which most of the villagers had by now graduated. I was to learn later that the reason why people called him 'poor old Hector' was because he had to live under the same roof as his virago of a sister, and when she died in unlikely circumstances in a ripeness of years I myself was destined to play an unlikely part in securing for old Hector a few final years of peace. But that's another story! Meantime I knew that whatever Hector's other faults might be, he was meticulous in his husbandry and he was always the first person in the village to have his winter peat-stack neatly secured at the end of his cottage. The idea of him plowtering through the moors looking for peat 'when the frost was cruel' was just too absurd for words, and so I abandoned my quest for a great truth in one of the world's best loved Christmas songs. I decided that if I was to indulge in fiction I would have fiction of my own choosing and so, while the others carolled and re-carolled, I resorted to surreptitiously reading my much-thumbed copy of *The Adventures of Dixon Hawke*. If the teacher noticed, she made sure she concealed her relief at being able to concentrate on her more promising choristers. I still can't sing *Good King Wenceslas* but I've still got a soft spot for him from those long years ago.

The first few weeks of preparation for the *Tret* (the word had now become accepted as a Gaelic one) were among the most contented of my school years. As the days wore on the need to conceal my detachment became less; every now and then I would look up and mime a few lines of whatever musical offering was being prepared for sacrifice and then I would return to whichever latest volume of *Dixon Hawke* I had been able to borrow. But then the teacher's enthusiasm took her by the scruff of the neck. One day, during normal school hours, she explained to us very carefully that Mrs Kerr came from another country (which we knew) and that that country had a National Anthem in the same way as our own country had a National Anthem (which we did not know) and that, as a big surprise for Mrs Kerr, we were secretly going to learn her native anthem and spring it on her at the end of the party.

I have had cause to reflect in the intervening years that poor Mrs Kerr had to conceal more than one emotion in the wake of that particular surprise, not least of which was that she had to accept having an alien nationality thrust upon her. We resumed friendship on an adult basis long years later and I learnt that though her maiden name had been Couvée, and though she had a French accent, she regarded herself as British as the Union Jack; and when the time came she chose to go back to her native Channel Islands to die. Perhaps if our 'surprise' had not been so well concealed she might have seized an early opportunity to correct the popular misconception as to her antecedents; but after that Christmas party she could no longer issue a disclaimer without causing embarrassment, and once she was enticed into bowing her head to the *Marseillaise* in public she was too late.

The shock of having discovered that there was a third language was equalled only by that of now finding myself in the situation of having to pronounce it. And there will always be for me a personal private agony in the words

Allons enfants de la patrie
Le jour de gloire est arrivé . . .

and all the rest of them. I was used to the idea of being unable to *sing* the words in a manner satisfying to anybody else, but being unable to *say* them was a totally new experience.

On the blackboard the words looked frightening enough but, at least, I could read them according to the laws of straight English. When it came to pronouncing them to the teacher's satisfaction, it was a different matter, because – to the surprise of all of us – it turned out that not only did she have a knowledge of the French language but a great love for it as well, and we went through painful hours while she tried to contort our vocal chords to produce noises for which nature had never intended them. We had only just mastered the art

12

of toning down our rolling Hebridean *r*s to the more genteel requirements of English; now we were being pressed to reproduce a smoother type of *r* altogether from some vague bit at the backs of our palates, and our native nasal 'honk' sounds which were deemed unsuitable for English were now very much in demand in French. The only gratifying thing from my point of view was that, in the general cacophony, my alleged tunelessness passed without comment and my confidence in my own vocal ability began to be restored. We must have rehearsed that blessed chunk of the *Marseillaise* many hundreds of times, while up in the old manse, indulging in a sip of champagne for all I know, Mrs Kerr was blissfully unaware of the surprise being prepared for her. And, down in the schoolhouse, the schoolteacher was equally blissfully oblivious to the fact that the surprise was going to be greater than she expected.

Chapter Two

I N compiling a story in the genre for which the distinguished Antipodean invented the description 'unreliable memoirs' I am keenly aware that many readers who know the Hebrides as natives of a younger generation, or as dedicated tourists visiting the islands under today's sophisticated conditions of transport or accommodation, may feel that I am writing of a place conjured out of a free-ranging imagination. But not so. While the tongue can't on occasion help but wander into the cheek, while memory can play false to details which are more the responsibility of the historian anyway, and while discretion – but much more frequently affection – makes me portray characters who have exchanged their own foibles with those of others, this is the new village substantially as it was at the time of the Christmas Treat.

Of the eight crofts which had been allocated to our ex-servicemen after the war, four had already had their modern stone-walled, slate-roofed, spacious houses built upon them with grants and loans from the Board of Agriculture, which, after many years of tentative effort, now seemed set to make small-farming in the shape of crofting into a viable way of life. Three crofts, including my father's, still had their original wood and corrugated iron temporary shacks on them; the one which had nothing at all on it belonged to a bachelor who wasn't in the same hurry to establish a solid base. So long as a man worked his land, no government pressure could be brought upon him in terms of when he had to build or what he had to build by way of family accommodation. In addition to the eight formal crofts, there were still a few landless cottars who lived on in their thatched black houses or had followed the lead of the incomers and put up what tended to be called shacks but were, in fact, small cosy homes lacking only in interior plumbing – which was not, after all, given very high priority even in Hebridean houses with more pretensions to grandeur than we had. What our community did have was a heart, unlike some more sophisticated mainland communities today, in the sense that we had, from the beginning, there awaiting us, a school, a church, and of course the old manse. And there it all was in a countryside of especial magic – a magic which is, in no way, the sentimental imagining of a nostalgic heart.

We looked poor to some of the travel writers who were beginning to seek us out with probing cameras and pens oozing purple prose; some of them made capital out of what they called our poverty because they didn't understand that poorness of amenity and lack of cash only represent poverty relative to the beholder's norms. Of course we looked poor to somebody from Mayfair in London or Morningside in Edinburgh. And we looked poor to socially conscious left wing observers like Louis MacNeice who wrote in *I crossed the Minch* about 'a row of poor shacks on the road to Leverburgh'. He was talking about us who were happy and contented – so far. What we did lack was pastime; because we were a new community, without time yet to build up a tradition, we didn't have the in-built traditional community recreations that had matured in old established Hebridean village societies whose folksong and lore were, even then, being archived; and, of course, the day of imported mechanical or pre-packed entertainment hadn't arrived. That was why simple occasions like the Christmas Treat assumed big proportions, and why little jokes got big laughs.

The *Tret* was, very nearly, not a laughing matter! It must have been loneliness, or the desire to be seen to be stretching out the hand of friendship, that prompted Mrs Kerr to invite every adult in the village to the last hour of the party. It was a wrong decision on every count!

The attitude of Western Islanders towards incomers into their communities can be ambivalent at the best of times, particularly if the incomer belongs to – or worse still, pretends to belong to – that strange upper category known as 'The County'! In recent years the attitude has begun to change, and 'the white settler' – as he has come to be called – is inclined to be judged on his merits and on his contribution to his adoptive community. But in those pre-war years, which were the years of my childhood, the islanders were regrettably prone to believe that God had allotted everybody a station in life and that the station of the English-speaking incomer was several rungs up the ladder of social order. There were two principal reasons for that. One was that the incomer (invariably able to buy and sustain a property for himself) was by sheer security and possession surer of himself – even in cases where he had not already had that self-assurance and 'apartness' instilled into him by his heredity or a public school education. We, on the other hand, were beginning to be aware of our lack of material possessions; and those grim generations of eviction and political repression had, unbelievably, left in us a lingering impulse to touch our foreheads to a 'bonnet laird'; there was even a trace of it still in our eight men – even in the ones who had come through Ypres and Mons and Arras, the Dardanelles and the rest.

Some incomers, and Mrs Kerr was one of them, tried hard to integrate into the community, and thought that to be like the people and *of* the people all they had to do was to acquire a smattering of Gaelic, or – at the very least – a Highland accent such as was being purveyed in the city music halls and on gramophone records by people like Harry Lauder. Mrs Kerr had found Gaelic to be quite beyond her, and – endowed as she was already with a French accent – she found it wellnigh impossible to superimpose a 'braw bricht moonlicht nicht' veneer on top of it; so she settled for pre-fixing every sentence with 'Ach well' and pronouncing 'just' *ch*ust. Life must have been very complicated for her because, when her own natural accent made her tend to refer to the more important points of the compass as *Norse* and *Souse*, our people thought that she was mimicking our English accents and they bridled! But, in truth, everybody liked her and felt sorry for her for having been left widowed and alone, and the majority thought that the invitation of the adults to the tail end of the Christmas Treat was a warm-hearted thought.

There were, of course, dissenters. Some people from 'the old village' and some from the neighbouring small township who were still loyal to the tenets of the Free Church or the Free Presbyterian Church disapproved of anything savouring of frivolity being conducted in a church manse – even if it was a Church of Scotland manse and, as such, smacking of Gomorrah. And the inclusion of the more mature citizens caused varying degrees of uneasiness in other quarters too. Our own incomer parents, while normally relishing anything suggestive of entertainment during a sullen winter, couldn't summon up much enthusiasm for dressing up in Sunday best for an occasion which threatened to be 'dry' in every sense of the word. The younger members of the school who had become more and more excited at the prospect of a beanfeast away from parental supervision, now found themselves with their enthusiasm dampening at the prospect of being supervised and drilled and criticized by proud parents. The 'big boys', as my buddies and I were now beginning to regard ourselves, with the pricklings of manhood beginning to make themselves felt, had been prepared to put up with the more formal aspects of the *Tret* for the sake of some surreptitious slap and tickle and the possibility of shuffling belly to belly with the meagre selection of female flesh available. Now suddenly we could see the whole thing disintegrating into a bib and tucker affair of *Grand Old Dukes of York* and interminable gatherings of *Nuts in May* such as we'd had to suffer at an occasional school soirée.

But there was no escape. As mid-December drew near, my mother's preoccupation with the *Tret* became obsessive; somehow or other the party had assumed new dimensions since she had confirmed that she could get somebody to keep an eye on the baby and allow her to have a rare evening out herself. Whatever occasional opportunities the menfolk might have had for getting away from the fireside during the winter, the womenfolk were, apart from the Sunday evening church service, almost totally housebound. Now, not only was she going out but she was going to go in the company of her offspring and they mustn't be allowed to disgrace her in public.

17

It didn't take her long to realize that there was nothing in the red trunk which served as a clothes store that was even remotely suitable for the elegant occasion that the *Tret* was threatening to become. It was a situation which didn't require much investigation since my total array of clothes consisted of two well-patched pairs of home-made Harris Tweed trousers and a couple of woollen ganzies from J. D. Williams or Oxendale. It was decided that I must have a suit. Not just a suit that would do me for the party but one which would see me through to summer when, as usual, I would be going to the Northlands to spend the entire school holiday with my grandparents – both lots of whom still lived there. The qualification about size was an unwelcome one because it meant that the suit was going to be large.

Fortunate people with overdrafts and access to a range of town shops may not see anything serious or complicated in the provision of a suit for a boy, but in a community where copper coins were counted, a junior suit was, invariably and of necessity, a matter of home construction. On the face of it the material should present no problem. Since the great Depression had begun to creep in on us – its grimy tentacles reaching out across the Minch from the cities and searching us out even in our remote corner – the Harris Tweed trade had collapsed, and yards upon yards of beautiful tweed that had been spun with toil and woven with high hope were now stacked unsold in every corner of the house, as symbolic of the times as the rusting hulks on Clydeside. My father had not aspired to a loom of his own yet so the unsold tweeds didn't just represent a stoppage of income; they stood for frozen investment, since he had had to pay the weaver out of the last of his meagre savings. But the store of tweeds couldn't be plundered at will to make a random suit for a seasonal party. The tweeds were of more or less standard lengths, and bits couldn't just be snipped off the ends of them; so my suit would obviously be selected from whatever range of offcuts remained, and the tweeds themselves carefully rolled back in their winding sheets till the economy resurrected and trade picked up again. In the end it turned out that very little was available. All the bits that I considered appropriate and attractive were either too small for the purpose in hand – 'might do for a pair of shorts later' – or else too big and 'might sell to a tourist for a sports jacket in summer'! I could see it coming. I could scarcely avoid it. Two and a half yards of garish experimentation which was the remainder of a suit length that had been specially commissioned by a half-cracked Tory politician who had been round canvassing votes for his hapless protégé in the 1935 General Election. I remembered that my father had said his taste in tweed was in the same place as his taste in politics – because I'd got into trouble for using the same phrase later – and I also remembered how his parsimony had been condemned when he had cut back his order from a suit length to a jacket length when the election had, predictably, avalanched in the wrong direction. And now here I was listening to the virtues of the rejected plus-fours being extolled to me! A large crotal-brown and blue double overcheck on a cream background. Fine for cushion covers or putting below the saddle of a horse, I protested vehemently. But not, please God, a suit. It was useless. I couldn't have a piece off the end of a crotal and white blend, or the herring-bone, or the dog-tooth . . . they would sell when things got better, and I might be able to get a bought suit out of one of the catalogues with some of the money from them. The arguments were still flying backwards and forwards as the huge pattern for an outsize suit was being traced on a sheet of brown paper on the table, and when the big scissors began to snip I knew that all was lost. But I couldn't foresee that worse was to come.

Two or three nights later somebody noticed that my hair was too long. There was nothing unusual about that and I didn't even suspect anything out of the ordinary when my brother sniggered. My mother was by way of being the village barber. A keen eye, an artistic touch, and a reputation for letting the scissors cut rather than pluck had established her prestige even with 'the bloods', our red-corpuscled hobblede-hoys who would come to her for a 'trum' before setting off in search of adventure in the neighbouring villages. I never minded a haircut from my mother; but I looked for a place to hide when she announced that the suit was her contribution to the *Tret*, and that the rest was up to my father. My father!

Whose only claim to experience in that direction was that he sheared forty blackfaced sheep every July.

It would be pointless to attempt to describe the result for somebody who didn't know the face below it. In the years since then various outlandish styles have come, have been welcomed or derided, and have gone. *Brando, Tony Curtis, Crew Cut, Punk* . . . they've all had their day, but mine fell somewhere between the one known now as *Skinhead* and the one known once upon a time as a *D.A.*

There is something irrevocable about a botched haircut. The word spoken in haste is heard only by a few and may be forgotten; the deed done in the dark may be forgiven; but the haircut lingers on for an eternity, reproachfully, like a tarnished halo for the world to comment on. And after that haircut had mercifully outgrown itself it was still to live on in the folklore for months while I was referred to as 'an convick' which is, approximately, the Gaelic pronunciation of the soubriquet for certain residents of Dartmoor and Peterhead. It was with very little self-confidence that there set out for the manse on that evening of 24 December a very large suit containing a very bald me.

The *Tret*, although it had been 'billed' for the manse, was actually convened in a vast outhouse which had been a dairy in the days when ministers kept cows and milkmaids. But it didn't look like a dairy any more. The windows had been beautifully draped with curtains from the manse drawing-room and even the walls were heavily festooned with gaily coloured travelling rugs and bedspreads with Celtic designs. At one end of the room a great peat fire was burning in the ingle round which, presumably, the minister's farm workers had congregated in winters of yore at times when the place wasn't being used as a dairy. A huge trelliswork had been erected from which hung streamers and gold and silver baubles that twinkled in the lamplight, and presents in parcels. The proceedings began with our rendering of *Good King Wenceslas*, which drew a hearty burst of applause from Mrs Kerr and her maid, and we were warned that we would have to do it again when the grown-ups arrived. Then there was dancing to a large cabinet gramophone into which Mrs Kerr kept feeding records. *The Grand Old Duke* marched up hill and down dale, bodies whirled and hooched slightly self-consciously in approximations of *Eightsome Reels*, and then *One Steps* and other close ones of which I had dreamt for nights but from which I now crouched sullenly in my corner in my suit. I could see my friends surreptitiously rubbing themselves up against Meg and Peggy and the other girl whom I can only remember by her shape, although every time she slouched past me I was stirringly aware of that indefinable smell of girl of which I'd been becoming more insistently conscious ever since Wee Sarah had kindled a spark that hadn't been strong enough to catch flame, that night that seemed so long ago. I hadn't seen Wee Sarah ever since and I didn't really want to; I knew that the moment had come before its time, but that sooner or later it would repeat itself with someone else even if I had to give opportunity a nudge.

After a sticky tea, small presents were handed out from the trellis which, I was to understand later, symbolized a Christmas tree in our treeless land; the wee ones needed no encouragement to demonstrate their enthusiasm for their toys, but the big ones had to be encouraged out of the side of her mouth by the teacher to simulate excitement as the torn wrappers revealed worthy books like *Coral Island*, the illustrated child's version of *Pilgrim's Progress* and *Milestones On My Way* – all of which carried little labels declaring that they had been donated by a worthy body called 'The Band of Hope' (for whose best known charity there was precious little demand in our bit of the kingdom in those days). I was one of the fortunate ones, landing a copy of *Coral Island*, and I was to derive a lot of pleasure from R. M. Ballantyne's little classic once I realized that his characters weren't all the goody-goodies that the lurid wrapper suggested. Despite myself my spirits were rising, and they soared when I saw everybody being presented with a false face amidst much hilarity. I stuck mine on and immediately felt that upsurge of self-assurance which character actors get from the layering of their make-up. But it was short-lived. I was beginning to chassé my way through the throng with my ardour rising and Meg firmly in my sights when the voice of my bosom crony and habitual partner in crime, Gillespie, piped in my ear, 'How's an convick?' and my enthusiasm chilled as I realized that the only bit of me I had concealed was the only bit that I didn't mind being seen.

Mrs Kerr clapped her hands for silence, and when she got it she announced that our Sunday School Certificates would be handed out when our parents arrived – as they should be doing in about half an hour's time – but would we all now please form a ring for *The Farmer Wants a Wife*? O God! There is no more emasculating charade for a self-conscious pubescent than that particular game, nor anything more designed to hold him up to ridicule if his particular weaknesses lie in the spheres of dancing and singing. I prayed that I would be the wretched bone and, thereby, be the last to be hauled into the centre of the ring – even if I knew that my friends would spare not an ounce of their energy when it came to thumping my new suit. But my whole instinct screamed at me that I would draw the short straw and be the farmer, stuck there in the middle of the ring for the eternity of the dance looking like somebody who hadn't even been dreamt of then – the scarecrow from Judy Garland's *Wizard of Oz*. My instinct was right. Miss Martin had obviously noticed that I had been keeping a low profile for most of the evening and she must have dreamt up some charitable reason of her own for my unwonted reticence. 'Finlay will be the farmer!' she shouted. 'In you go, convick,' hissed Gillespie as a dozen hands pushed me into the centre and somebody struck up the inane recitative as they all began to twirl round me. I was grateful that my mask at least hid the red blood that was puffing my face, and concealed the fact that I wasn't joining in the singing. Whatever other enthusiasms I had been nurturing were banished emphatically, as I shuffled from leg to leg in imitation of a solo Highland dancer and the fearsome hairiness of Harris Tweed especially designed for leathery deer-stalkers and hillwalkers began to take its chafing toll of my thighs and every other part of me that it could reach. In a fit of defiance I seized on a toothless little mite from the Lower Infants when the moment came for the farmer to choose a wife, and I didn't give a hoot for the shouts of derision from my own classmates with whom I'd been exchanging boasts for weeks. The little girl, who had shed her mask somewhere, looked up at me in gummy adoration and I think I loved her for the innocence which blinded her to my tonsure and my tweed. The game was grinding to its inexorable climax as the door opened and the village began to shuffle in.

We had been swopping apprehensions in school from the day we heard that the adults were to be invited but, contrary to our worst fears, the night burst into life when they arrived. I suspect that they had been girding themselves for a grim evening, and the result was that they put all their efforts into preventing it from going that way; either that, or the false faces with which they were issued by Mrs Kerr and Miss Martin – with much giggling and coy little asides to the men – gave them the kind of self-confidence that mine failed so signally to give me. Mrs Kerr began to dole out lemonade to all and sundry and people tipped back their false faces like visors to drink; the men proclaimed hearty toasts and drained their glasses as if they contained champagne – which, come to think of it, they may have done! Music erupted as our hostess fed a more adult record into the cabinet gramophone and the celebrations took off. Men who couldn't, danced with their own and their neighbours' wives; those who reckoned they could, queued up to partner Mrs Kerr – presumably deluded into thinking that their wives could be persuaded to believe that they were duty dancing, or else that they couldn't be recognized behind their papier-mâché alter egos. The only person who didn't dance was old Hector MacGeachan who had screwed up his courage and decided that his sister could harangue or ail in solitude to her heart's content; Hector had been given an express personal invitation by Mrs Kerr, and he was given a seat of honour at the fire. And it was Mrs Kerr in person who stuck a bearded false face on him during a pause between dances and, giggling a lot as she was doing that night, dug into his pocket and produced his old pipe and stuck it into his mouth. 'There you are, Mr MacGeachan,' she said. 'You light up and enjoy yourself. . .' but before she could say anything else another father grabbed her by the waist and whirled her away into an old-fashioned waltz or something equally intimate.

Old Hector may or may not have wanted to smoke, but he

23

was one of those whose forefathers had suffered from the landlord purge and he himself was descended from three generations of ghillies. It was in his blood, therefore, to do whatever he was bidden to do by anybody whom he considered to be his superior, and some people used to claim unkindly that he would take an order from a tinker's donkey if it was in English. It wasn't true. Old Hector was a kindly man who would suffer hurt himself rather than hurt anybody else, but I doubt if he held the centre of any stage till that night . . . or till the last few years of which he hadn't yet as much as dreamt. Anyway he began to part the long white whiskers on the false face so that he could better manoeuvre his pipe into his mouth, and he began to feel through his pockets for the old page of newspaper which he always carried with him for spills. He found it just as the dance ended and as the teacher, indiscreetly showing a knee, climbed on to a chair and called for silence. 'Ladies and gentlemen,' she said in her best classroom voice. 'Before we all get carried away with ourselves we must express our thanks to Mrs Kerr for her great kindness, and I think the children and I can best do so in a little surprise that we have prepared for her!' I knew that the moment had come for the dreaded *Allons enfants de la . . .*

But it wasn't just Mrs Kerr who was in for a surprise!

Unnoticed by anybody, Hector MacGeachan had lit a large spill of newspaper and, in the process of negotiating it towards his pipe, he had set the beard of his false face on fire. Not badly, but on fire. Without wishing to disturb anybody, and with great presence of mind, he had removed his false face (probably acting more quickly than he had done since he had gaffed his last salmon many years before) and had flung it into a corner where, unhappily, it had set fire to one of the damask curtains that had been commandeered from the manse drawing-room. Smoke was eddying round the room when Mrs Kerr noticed it and shouted 'Fire!' – without waiting to establish whether or not this was the surprise that the teacher had in store for her.

The effect of that word is universally dramatic, but probably never anywhere more so than in a room crowded with mothers frantically searching for their own offspring in a melée looking devilishly the same. There were only two calm females in the room and, for once in her life, one of them was my own mother. She had no problem identifying me, and we could see that my father already had my younger brother by the hand. And there was the devout old Widow Montgomery who had always maintained that no good would come of celebrating a Romish festival. As the room emptied she sat on in her chair, rocking backwards and forwards, and chanting 'For behold the Lord will come with fire to render His anger with fury, and His rebuke with flames. . . .'

Somehow we all found ourselves on the lawn whither Mrs Kerr and a couple of men had carried the burning curtain and stamped it out. Our hostess hadn't for an instant panicked but she now stood looking slightly forlorn and bemused, wondering perhaps what she could do with one damask curtain. My father took me by the shoulder and began to lead me away, but the voice of the teacher rang out and stopped us. 'Children!' she shouted, 'All's well that ends well. But though we've had an exciting evening we mustn't forget our surprise for Mrs Kerr!' And she signalled us to group around her while our hostess stood looking as if she'd had enough surprise to last her a lifetime. But when the teacher shouted 'One. Two. Three . . .' and we struck up the *Marseillaise* she stood very still and tried to look patriotic. The rest of the company shuffled and looked questioningly at each other – except for eight men who didn't hesitate before standing stiffly to attention.

A few hasty 'good nights' were mumbled, and as we made our ways quietly down the path to the new village road a delicate flutter of snow began to come down, as if somebody with a sense of humour was throwing a handful of confetti, or giving Mrs Kerr a gentle reminder about the Sunday School Certificates.

Chapter Three

B Y morning a thin coverlet of snow had draped itself over the village. Not the kind of snow which sends mainland boys rollicking into campaigns of snow fights and their seniors flapping up mountainsides risking coronaries in order to come slithering down again on skis at further risk to life and limb. We rarely got that kind of heavy fall because of being on the Atlantic's edge, and – although it could be cold – it was a damp kind of cold that we were accustomed to; the sort of cold on which rheumatism and chestiness thrived till the Hebrides took their gigantic leap forward into the realms of central heating in the last twenty or thirty years and creature comfort ceased to be regarded as a weakness of the flesh or the spirit. I have often wondered how dramatically the life of my own island of Harris would have been changed if the new village of my boyhood had been able to sustain its original momentum, if a world depression hadn't slowed up a hinterland which is always slower to recover, and if the amenities of which we kept hearing and reading had been available to us on our own home territory instead of beckoning us far afield like a tawdry grail. Perhaps the population of the island wouldn't have dropped by a third – as it has done in my lifetime – and perhaps I would have been there rather than here writing about it. But, for the boy getting up late on that winter's morning, the world held only the future and the great beauty of the snow.

I stood in my shirt-tails at the window looking out on it, conscious of its beauty without revelling in it, because the country boy grows up to accept nature as part of his due inheritance just as the country man grows not to notice it till it turns against him. I loved the rocky Northlands in which I'd been born and brought up for a few years – and to which I went back from time to time – but, because the Southlands had come as a surprise to me when I first glimpsed them, as we topped the Back of Scarista Hill on that first day when the village became ours, the meld of beach and sea and mountain never lost its magic for me, nor its ability to surprise. Here it was now, yet again different. The machair that had been warm with daisies in the summer was now bleached white with the rime of the snow and I was thinking to myself that that was what the Holy Land must have been like, judging by the few Christmas cards that I had seen, despite the fact that my reading in school seemed to suggest a climate that made snow unlikely. I had long since given up asking the teacher questions about the discrepancies between her gospel teachings in the morning and her geography teaching in the afternoon.

'You'd better put your trousers on if you're thinking of going out,' my father said as he came in from the byre with the milkpails. 'Your brother's out there with a snowman as big as himself!'

'Of course I'll put my trousers on,' I said with as much asperity as I could risk. 'I'm not going out yet!' I wondered why he had taken to doing the morning milking; if we hadn't already got a fairly new baby I might have suspected that my mother was succumbing to the fresh epidemic of maternity which was sweeping the village. But no. The idea was ridiculous.

'And don't forget to put something on your head before you go out.'

I bit my lip hard and stared straight out of the window. I hadn't spoken to him ever since he had given me the haircut two nights ago. I had been very skilful about it. I had been disarmingly obedient and had performed any little chores demanded of me with no demur; I had kept my looks from being insolent; I had been utterly charming to my mother. But I had studiously avoided addressing one single remark to my father or reacting to any comments of his; I knew that he knew, and I knew that he knew why. And now I had fallen for a sucker punch because my mind had been wandering idly over the more pleasant aspects of last night's party (which really boiled down to the fire) and the compelling beauty of the snow. I didn't have to turn round because I could tell from the way he was whistling tunelessly that he was stifling a smile. My father and I had developed a marvellous relationship which puberty, paradoxically, was strengthening rather than abrasing. He had an extraordinary love of books and a sensitive feeling for poetry, both of which he was unobtrusively instilling in me and which, in turn, resulted in the bond which was undoubtedly there – although there was precious little evidence of it that morning. In fact, a further resentment – which I had almost let slip – was at the fact that he had collared *Coral Island* as soon as we got home from the *Tret* and I hadn't seen it since. Now certainly was not the time to ask him about it, so I turned on my heel, dashed past him into the bedroom, pulled on my trousers and ganzie, and ran out to join my brother at his snowman. My brother was getting to the stage where he could provide good companionship when Gillespie wasn't around, but he didn't have Gillespie's sophistication nor the supply of dirty stories and vocabulary that Gillespie was forever gleaning from older cousins of his. Not the least of the failings of the educational system of the time was that my brothers and I had, perforce, to leave home at an early age for our higher education – and so we were men before we became friends.

It was Donald who noticed Calum the Post's van coming into the village. There had been doubt whether there would be a Post at all since it was Christmas Day, but no holidays were mandatory as far as Calum was concerned and the general consensus had been that he wouldn't miss out on the pre-Hogmanay hospitality which was now beginning to seep through, and that he would choose to take a day in lieu at peat-cutting or sheep-shearing time. There he was now, staggering up to the manse, laden with parcels.

'I wonder if he'll have a parcel for us?' My brother was an optimist, and I told him so. The most we could hope for in the way of Christmas correspondence was a Greetings Card or two from some mainland cousins of my father or mother. The increasing burden of Christmas mail which Calum had begun to grumble about in the early thirties had receded, although we as children didn't attach any significance to it; but what *was* increasing, peculiarly enough, was the volume of advertising mail as the entrepreneurs of the cities began to discover our existence. Charles Atlas was offering to build Hebridean muscles; compilers of encyclopaedias were volunteering to fortify our minds; Glaxo were eager to build bonnie babies, happily unaware that all they were building in Harris was a repertoire of ribald jokes. Whenever I found an advertisement with a postage pre-paid coupon I sent it off, just for the fun of having Calum stop at the roadside gate with a letter addressed to me personally, and all the older boys and girls in school did the same.

One or two of them got into serious trouble with their parents when they went on to commit themselves to courses offered by sundry body-builders for sums greater than one would expect to pay a contractor for a modest house, but they always got extricated by the teacher – who had a great talent for writing to the vendors letters which made their actions sound criminal. She sometimes ended up with token little gifts from them for sparing them from legal action which she had had no intention of instigating and in which they would, in any case, have been proved totally innocent if slightly imbecilic for being taken in by semi-literate Gaelic-speaking boys and girls in the Western Isles. I am sure that only as a final resort some city executive would glance at a map and look away in hasty horror on discovering that he had been spending his company's resources on specks of islands in the Atlantic where the natives probably wore marram skirts.

One triumphant advertiser was a Mr Alexander Kennedy of Glasgow. Mr Kennedy, in the late twenties or early thirties, had gone into the laundry and dyeworks business, for which he found a lucrative and expanding demand in Glasgow. But not content with that he decided to push his frontiers nationwide and right out into the Outer Hebrides where professional laundry did not come high on the list of priorities. Mr Kennedy was obviously perfectly well aware of that, and his campaign was directed at the future. He formed the *Castlebank Children's Circle*, with its headquarters at (and the address is indelibly imprinted on my mind from all those years ago) *Castlebank Dyeworks, Anniesland, Glasgow*. For no membership fee, except the signed promise to be a loyal member, a youngster enrolled in the CCC and got a certificate of membership and a beautiful enamelled badge of a knight in black armour on a black horse in front of a turreted castle. I have no idea now what the significance was; I am reasonably sure that suits of armour and horses and castles did not come within the scope of Mr Kennedy's laundering and dyeing facilities. Every child in our school became an accredited member of the *Castlebank Children's Circle*, and in exchange we became eligible to compete in painting competitions, essays, and puzzles of all descriptions for which there were reasonably generous little prizes. The activities of the club were so varied and involved such a wide range of general knowledge that even the brightest of us had to involve the assistance of parents and school to an extent that could well have justified an honorary senior club membership with an appropriate enamel badge to match. All of us involved in the ever increasing ordeals of tests and examinations in school probably owed more than a few marks to Mr Kennedy; we certainly owed him a great deal of our general knowledge, and had he been alive today he would probably have qualified for a grant from the Arts Council. Or the Arts Council might have received a grant from him. By the time I came to live in the city, and moved into realms where dry cleaning and laundering were normal routines of life, it would have been as instinctive for an otter to pass by a salmon as for me to bypass one of the innumerable Castlebank laundries. I regret not one penny of mine that went to swell into millions the take-over value of his business a few years ago; my only regret was that I never met him, although he and I lived only a mile or two apart in the city for many years. He might have smiled to be told that his was the only Christmas card that Calum the Post had for my brother and myself that day, that year long ago, and that it brightened life for a whole family.

Calum was in an evil temper as Donald and I joined my father at the red van. I automatically assumed that the purple language sizzling the frosty Christmas air was directed at one of his usual targets – the Bolsheviks, Hitler or Franco. 'Mark my words, we're heading for a war,' he used to thunder at my father. 'And you and I'll be in it. We're the very kind they'll want – men with experience. If my mother was alive I'd ask her to her face if I was born in a bloody uniform; I've never been out of one anyway. . . .'

But the warmongers were not the objects of his venom that day; it was 'that bloody woman', who turned out to be Mrs Kerr. 'I'd hoped to be home early today; the wife's roasting a cockerel seeing it's Christmas, or supposed to be anyway, and there's hardly any mail. Now I've got to stop at every damn house in the place to deliver *these*, just because I was fool enough to take a glass of piss-tasting sherry and a sixpence before I realized what she was up to.' With that he thrust into my hand, past my father, the two envelopes containing Alexander Kennedy's Christmas cards and a large square piece of ornate pasteboard showing a picture of what I took to be a couple of crofters labouring on a Hebridean croft, or they might be a couple of Galileans labouring in a Galilean vineyard. In either case it is still my certificate to prove that I attended a Sunday School regularly and with good conduct, although – struggle as I may with my memory – I haven't the faintest recollection of ever having attended Sunday School in my life.

'My, my, Calum was on the bow today,' my father said when he finally joined us in the house where my mother was admiring the Castlebank Christmas cards and setting them out on the brass fringed mantelpiece above the stove, in between ornate tea caddies on which King George V and Queen Mary were celebrating their silver jubilee, Edward VIII was celebrating nothing in particular, and King George VI had pride of place because he had been crowned along with an honest Scottish woman with a good Highland name. Divers reminders of the great moments of human glory and tragedy and dignity, events that had set the world by the ears and passed us by with scant notice in our once hopeful new world, now encapsulated on a simple little shelf edged with sixpence worth of brass. 'I think it must have been the sherry that did for poor Calum. If Mrs Kerr had given him a good dram of whisky it would have been all right, don't you think Finlay?'

'I don't know,' I replied.

'But for sure he wouldn't have delivered the Christmas cards if Mrs Kerr hadn't given him the certificates to hand round. She must have forgotten to hand them out last night in the stramash!' I noticed the twinkle in his eye, and remembered that I wasn't talking to him. But it was too late; he had got the better of me again. There was an unmistakable smell of fruit dumpling coming from a pot on the fire, and my common sense told me that it would be churlish to keep up my resentment when mother was obviously trying to mount some little token celebration of the day.

'Big fellow, what about coming up the hill with me? I'll have to go for a bag of peat with Sunday coming up tomorrow. In the excitement of getting ready for that party I forgot to bring home an extra bag and, in any case, I wasn't to foresee that it was going to snow today. Perhaps you could manage a half bag yourself, eh?'

The reference to the hill and the snow in the same breath would have sounded inconsequential to a stranger, but I guessed what he meant and I felt a little flattered to be considered in the role that he had cast for me. He had a wholesome respect for the hills, and although Bleaval was by no means the cruellest of our mountains it was a fairly steep climb up the riverside track to the shoulder where our best peatbanks lay. It was just a foot-wide path which he had worn out himself over the years, taking advantage of rabbit and sheep tracks where he could. Every second day in life he had climbed up, filled a hundredweight sack of peat, and – tying it round his shoulders with a twist of coir rope – had trudged back down with it again. Once one learnt how to pack the sack so that sharp edges of peat didn't dig into the spine, and once one had got the knack of placing the fulcrum and distributing the weight it wasn't as burdensome as it sounds; but it was bad enough, and for the life of me I have never been able to figure out why he had never invested in a horse or a pony which would have lightened the work on the croft in a hundred different ways. I can only imagine that it was because he was a Northman and wasn't used to horses. One of the most exasperating things about the crofters of our place and that generation was that they were reluctant to adapt to even the most tested of labour-saving tactics. Those who did were the ones who survived. The reason my father wanted me with him on the hill that day was that he knew that, higher up the hill, the conditions would be worse and that a simple slip and a twisted ankle could land a man alone with a heavy load on his back in trouble, and lead to endless trouble for others. He was practising the preaching that pleasure hill-walkers ignore so often, and so often to their cost.

We walked slowly up the hill together, pausing now and then to look back down over the village from which the peat smoke was rising as straight as a pencil from each house. 'It's going to be a fine day tomorrow. Frosty perhaps, but fine. There's no surer sign than the smoke rising straight up. It's the same idea as a barometer, you know. . .' and on he went feeding me knowledge in the guise of chit-chat. And then he got on to his favourite topic of the old stone ruins more clearly visible than usual with the light snow on the winter heather. 'They're not all eviction houses you know. Some of these were summer houses built here when the place consisted of a few large farms; in the summer the milking cows used to graze on the hills without coming back down to the machair at all, and instead of calling them home for milking in the evening as our women do because they've only got a couple of cows each to deal with, the milkmaids used to come out and spend weeks on the moors in these huts, making the milk into butter and crowdie and pressing the crowdie into cheese. Then from time to time the men would come out and carry the salted butter and the cheese home and store it for the winter. Good stones, these. We might find a way of getting some of them down to the croft when we come to building the new house.'

My interest brightened.

'The new house? When are we going to start?' I'd begun to become conscious of our cramped living quarters; I relished the freedom of my grandfather's grand two storey house in the Northlands; and I was getting envious of those of my school-friends whose fathers had already moved into their 'white houses'.

He took his time to answer. 'O I don't know. Maybe we'll begin collecting stones soon.' A strange distant look came into his eyes whenever he mentioned the business of collecting stones for the new house. 'The country's in a bad way just now and money's scarce for grants and loans. But I don't know why you're bothering anyway. You'll be sitting your bursary next year and you'll be getting away from here. Another three years and Donald will be going away. And in no time it'll be Alex's turn. . . .'

'The baby? It'll be ten years before he's sitting the bursary! And, in any case, we'll be coming back.'

'Aye, maybe. You never know how things go. There was a time when I never thought I'd be coming back here, when I was working in Glasgow. But the war changed that. And the way things are looking there'll be another war before all that long.'

He changed the conversation.

I didn't notice it of course, but the relentless conditioning of the mind was going on, perhaps subconsciously on his own part. Phrases like 'you'll be getting away from here' and 'I never thought I'd be coming back here' passed unnoticed over my immediate understanding, but he had mentioned the bursary again and that reminded me that the bursary examination was, indeed, not so very far away. It had been drummed into me as the first great hurdle of my life, and by now I had accepted that one of those coveted County Council awards was the only key to success and prosperity. In my own mind I had decided that I must win.

When we reached the peat stack he packed a fairly full bag of peat for me, and taught me how to sit down on the edge of the raised bank and get the sack balanced on my shoulders. 'Don't tie the rope,' he said as he put it round the bag and gave me the loose ends to grip. 'Just hold the ends tightly, and that way you'll automatically let it go if you stumble and you'll come to no harm. We don't want you strangling yourself before your hair grows.' That way the subject of the haircut passed smoothly into the realms of humour, and, indeed, I found that the full bag of peat carefully balanced was a much easier heft than a half full bag gripped over a shoulder by its neck and swinging round my buttocks.

'What about you and me going to church tomorrow? It might be a nice idea seeing it's the day after Christmas.'

He must have taken my silence, as I concentrated on the footpath, for demur.

'You wouldn't have to wear your suit,' he added. 'Your old trousers and ganzie would do fine.'

So the whole matter was settled without my having much say in it, nor yet being made to feel pressurized in any way. By the time we got home, the old closeness was back, and the little house, warm in the lamplight, had about it a great feeling of what I was in later years to come to know as Christmas. After we'd eaten as much currant dumpling as we could stow away we all sat quietly round the stove. Resignedly, I went back to *Dixon Hawke* – which I was beginning to know off by heart – while my brother thumbed through the picture book that he'd been given at the *Tret*, and my father puffed contentedly at his pipe, having dug *Coral Island* out of a corner where I'd never thought of looking. My mother knitted and smiled contentedly as she looked round her brood.

Church next forenoon was bleak and cold. Ancient stone takes a lot of warming up at the best of times, but our huge church had little warmth to retain from the bodies of the 30 people who sat in its cavernous emptiness once a week for an hour and a half. Having no minister of our own, our less urgent spiritual needs, including the Sunday morning service, were attended to by the man whose designation was 'missionary' – a title dating back to the middle of the eighteenth century when, indeed, missionaries had been sent to help 'civilize' the Highlands after Culloden in much the same way, and with much the same motive, as missionaries were despatched to darkest Africa and other anonymous fringes of the Empire. The Highland ones were safe from the danger of being eaten, but, in all other respects the early ones must have felt their purpose to be the same – to lead His people out of darkness to the feet of a stern and unforgiving God, who would, in His own good time, forgive them their sins and their rebelliousness against the Establishment. By our time, of course, the role of the missionary had changed although his title had not. He was now really a lay preacher, an ex-shepherd or fisherman who had seen the Light and felt confident enough to lead others through the gloom. They had good precedents in fishermen and shepherds and, as in former days, the system threw up some very powerful men; preachers who could, by sheer oratory and belief launch religious revivals which swept the land. Others had an undoubted sufficiency of holiness, and a doubtful sufficiency of grammar.

Having deposited our penny and halfpenny respectively in the wooden plate at the door, father and I made our echoey way down the flagged aisle to our seat. Although the whole congregation could have crowded for warmth into two seats at the very most, the code of the family pew was strictly observed and our pew (the eighteenth down on the right if I remember rightly) was the one which had been occupied by the Clerics, my father's ancestors on his mother's side, for the best part of two hundred years. By taking his place there when he came to the new village he was, in his own romantic heart, picking up the threads of the traditions of a lineage of which he was very proud. There were two beautiful oak pulpits, one above the other, at the altar end of the church, and when there was a fully qualified minister in charge of the service he occupied the top pulpit and the precentor, who led the singing, occupied the lower one. No mere missionary, however, would dare occupy the top pulpit; his humility didn't allow him climb so near to God as the man entitled to the round collar, and so the precentor was demoted to ground level while the missionary took the lower pulpit. That day the precentor (one of the crofters from the village next to ours) was already in his place, but the missionary hadn't arrived and nobody was quite sure who he was going to be. After ten minutes or so of throat-clearing and feet-shuffling we heard him coming heavily down the aisle, with the slow solemn tread of the presbyterian who thinks he is carrying the Almighty on his shoulders instead of the other way round, and as he passed the end of the pew I heard my father mutter below his breath a heart-wrung 'O God, no!' I knew that things were not promising.

The service started and followed its usual pattern – the style still followed in most Western Island churches – with the audience sitting to sing and standing to pray. My father couldn't sing and I know not what he prayed, but whatever it was he had plenty of time to do it; even my young legs were aching by the time we got sitting down. At least I enjoyed the singing, because it was the easiest of all types in my reckoning; the precentor 'gave out' each line of psalm and the congregation chanted it with him when he repeated it, with the few who could claim good voices grace-noting the musical lines. There are few more moving experiences than being in among a large Gaelic congregation singing in the traditional manner with soul and feeling. It is more than moving; it is unforgettable in the depths of one's being. There is a discernible gap between that and the paean achieved by 30 self-conscious souls in a miniature cathedral, frozen to the marrow and bored to extinction.

I knew that my father was impatient for the sermon to start and, when at long last the missionary got round to it, father's head went down on his folded hands on the narrow ledge in front of him with a sigh of relief. He always did it. And he had always assured me that it was because he had to shut out the view from the spacious windows because his mind wandered. He hadn't expected me to believe him, so he didn't regard it as lying. Today was different. I had just got nicely engrossed in trying to decipher some initials carved on the pew in front of me when I heard a distinct and satisfied-sounding snore. For a horrified second I fancied that the preacher had broken the rhythm of his monotony and was going to address a remark directly to my father but, to my relief, he carried on. I kicked my father sharply in the region of the ankle and he sat up with a start. He looked balefully at me, collected his wits, confirmed for himself that the situation was as bad as he had feared, and put his head back down on his hands. In a few minutes he was snoring again. I kicked him again, and again he went through the exact same range of reactions, except that his glare at me was even more explicit. But it didn't matter; I couldn't bear the thought of a public rebuke from the pulpit – which was not at all an unheard of occurrence – and a missionary of insecure

37

self-importance was more likely to indulge his authority than an experienced minister. But it was a blessing in disguise. My preoccupation with my father passed the time for me, and I developed a refined technique of being able to kick him on the deep exhalation which I had come to recognize as the precursor to the snore. Mercifully the sermon drew to its close, the last prayer was said, and the last psalm sung with me happily unaware that it was virtually the end of my dream of myself as a vocalist of potential that people were merely being slow to appreciate.

Normally the end of the church service was followed by a long and leisurely exchange of news and views in which the visiting preacher would often take part, bringing reports of goings-on in other parts of the island. Most usually of late the conversation was on political lines and on the more and more familiar themes of Bolshevism and Fascism and all the *-isms* for which there appeared to be no Gaelic. That day the colloquium was much shorter, because people were frankly worrying about burnt dinners. One sentence reached me, as I stood on the fringe of the group, and it stirred some considerable alarm in me. George MacLellan, who was a staunch Liberal and inordinately proud of it, said something like 'We're having our own Bolshevik here if what they tell me is true. . .' and the rest of what he said was lost on me as people hurried to get away before the preacher emerged.

'What's a Bolshevik?' I asked as we walked down hill.

'A Bolshevik. O, a kind of revolutionary. . .' he broke off and shook me good humouredly by the shoulder. 'That reminds me; that was a very dangerous thing you did in church today. You should never give a man a fright when he's sleeping. . . .' And there followed a long and colourful story of the French Revolution. Apparently when the bloodshed was at its height, a lady with Royalist sympathies, terrified for her life, went to church with her maid. Even in the midst of her distress, weariness overcame the lady as she tried to concentrate on the preacher, and she fell asleep and had a fearful dream that she was being made to kneel beneath the guillotine. Just as the blade was about to descend, her maid, horrified, noticed that her mistress was asleep and, in order to waken her, tapped her smartly on the back of the neck with her fan. Whereupon the poor woman, taking the tap of the fan to be the blade of the guillotine, fell down dead. The story was very dramatically told and lasted all the way home. It was guaranteed to ensure that I would never waken him in church again, but at the same time I had received a preliminary little lesson about the French Revolution so that when I did, years later, come up against Robespierre and company they didn't come as complete strangers to me.

'But what's a Bolshevik revolutionary person coming to this village for?' I asked as we reached the gate.

'O that? What Geordie MacLellan was talking about? I'm not sure, but I think she's going to bring about one of the biggest revolutions of all; she's going to teach you to sing!'

She? A Bolshevik? A revolutionary? Going to teach me to sing? It didn't make sense, and it was obvious that he didn't know any more. It was also obvious that I was going to have to wait for the school holidays to pass before I would find out.

Chapter Four

WE could be very cruel. The Gaelic word for 'feet' is 'casan', and so we called the new music teacher 'Miss Casan' because we reckoned that she had three feet. She didn't, of course! The poor woman had a deformity which looked like a tiny foot protruding from one shin bone, and because her name was Bassin and rhymed neatly with 'casan' she was landed with an allonym which was as unworthy as it was unkind. In later years Ethel Bassin was to become a good friend of mine, and the more I got to know her the more I admired her courage and her musicianship and her tenacity. Of the last quality there is no greater proof than that it took her five years to accept that she couldn't teach me to sing. From the beginning she was intrigued and, indeed, bemused by the phenomenon of somebody who could produce each note in the scale with alarming confidence, but could not *re*produce them in any required or pre-ordained order, which – after all – is the most basic requirement in the aspiring singer's art.

Music has been a torment for me all my adult life, and an ungenerous Divinity has ruled that it should be my lot to live out my time in an environment ringing with musicians. One eminent one is my dearest friend, generous in every respect save one; when the jokes have all been told and the night is wearing thin he will invariably try to rekindle the merriment by recalling some aged anecdote involving me and my infirmity (as he manifestly regards it), whereupon the company erupts into interest which varies from incredulity to demands that I demonstrate my incapacity as if I were a circus freak. But such occasions are, at least, normally private. The much greater punishment is to have been born into a nation hell-bent on singing "Auld Lang Syne" once after meals and twice before bedtime, and it pains me to remember the number of excellent, well-oiled top table dinners that have been ruined for me by having to attempt to stand at the end between two enthusiastic dinner jackets, miming with feigned feeling the words

And there's a hand my trusty fiere
And gie's a hand o' thine!

while long tablefuls of ears seem to be straining to catch my every syllable. But for Miss Bassin they might be getting more entertainment than they bargained for!

By the time Miss Bassin had arrived, as the first of a new breed of invading itinerant teachers of the fine arts, our village school had settled down into a cosy community of 13 – a figure at which it seemed to remain static for two or three years with new raw recruits arriving from time to time to replace the slightly less raw 'seniors' who moved on to the realms of higher education or else moved out at the age of fourteen to take their places in the society of the village where they would, invariably, stay only till such time as they got a chance to get away to some mainland job. A *chance* to get away! For all her good points – and they were many – Miss Martin could not get away from the intellectual malaise of her generation; to 'get away' was synonymous with success; to stay and build on the promising foundations of a new village was failure. But at least she did ensure that everybody who went through her school in her time had a grounding in general knowledge far beyond the formal bounds of the official curriculum. She taught the boys to cook and sew. She taught the girls the rudiments of gardening. She taught us all to follow world events in the newspapers and, later, on the radio. And she taught everybody to sing – except me!

From tenderest infancy I was convinced that the art of singing was a simple matter of striking a high falsetto and rendering a lyric *con amore* and *fortissimo*, and nobody had ever informed me to the contrary. The only instruction I had ever received at home was 'to be quiet'. When the teacher first produced a modulator and a tuning fork I found the whole business of rattling through from one 'doh' to another singularly boring, and I was glad when I was left to my own devices while she concentrated on select pupils like Gillespie, who seemed to be having difficulties with 'fah', 'me', and 'ray', short simple words though they were.

I came into my own – to my own satisfaction at least – when we moved on to actual songs, even although the choice was not often very inspiring. As with everything else, music was taught in English and the repertoire – presumably dictated by the same central authority that supplied the one and only book – ranged from "The Lass of Richmond Hill" to "I'll go no more a-roving". The young child learning a song or a poem will, inevitably, seek to relate its content with a place or a situation within the sphere of his own knowledge and, at the best of times, that can create its own problems; but the problems are compounded for the child dabbling in a language which is not his own. As far as we were concerned, Richmond Hill, wherever it was, must surely correspond to one of the tall heather-clad mountains surrounding the village on three sides, and a lass attempting to live on one of them even on a May day morn must have needed her head examined. And why, having painstakingly learnt that 'ruin' was pronounced 'ruin', were we now expected to pronounce it 'roo-aye-in' just because it was set to music? Truly the ways of English song were strange, and it was probably just as well that it was only during the last week of term or on the eve of a mid-term break that it was inflicted on us at all. That is, till Miss Bassin stumped onto the scene.

If the teacher knew of the impending visit she certainly did not inform us, and the first we knew of it was when the door burst open and an amply proportioned lady of incredible volubility demanded that two boys go out to her hire car and bring in her piano. We had seen a piano in the manse, and the idea of a car big enough to contain one was as incongruous as the notion of two boys being able to carry it. There was a rush for the door but it was quickly checked by the newcomer whose very tone was enough to warn us that here was somebody whom it would be foolhardy to contradict. 'Two, I said. It's not the car I want brought in!' And the two boys nearest the door slunk out, to reappear a few minutes later with something that looked for all the world like a miniature coffin, which she ordered to be laid across two desks while a third boy was detailed to place a chair in front of it. After a few minutes of conversation with the teacher the latter, looking rather relieved, left the room and headed for her own living quarters, presumably to prepare tea, leaving us to the mercies of Miss Bassin who, we were informed, would be teaching us music for an hour every Thursday afternoon for the foreseeable future. Teaching us! This was putting music on a new plane. Up till now music had been supposed to be fun even if it provided little in the way of laughs.

The newcomer sat down to her box-of-tricks and, when she opened it, there sure enough was a row of black and white ivories with the black ones arranged in twos and threes just like the black ones on the black and yellow keyboard in the manse. And as if to prove the pedigree of her kist the lady brushed off a couple of arpeggios before turning to us and demanding to know the extent of our repertoire. It didn't take long to recite. "The Lass of Richmond Hill", "I'll go no more a-roving", "A rose-bud by my early walk", "Marching through Georgia" and, as the list petered out an infant voice lisped "In and out the dirty blue-bells", causing a ripple of laughter which subsided under the steely gaze through the pebble glasses. For what I was later to learn must have been one of the few times in her life, Miss Ethel Bassin was speechless.

'What . . .' she said, 'what about Gaelic songs?'

'What *about* Gaelic songs?' said our silence.

'What Gaelic songs have you been learning?' she said slowly, thinking that her first question hadn't got through to us.

Silence.

'What about. . .?' And she proceeded to accompany herself in a rendering of "The Eriskay Lovelilt" in passable if slightly fractured Gaelic.

No, we hadn't heard it. No, we didn't learn Gaelic songs.

That, she assured us, would be remedied. But, first of all, she must establish our various capabilities. And she began to tinkle out little runs of notes which we were all invited to reproduce as 'la-la-la-tum-tetee-tum-tetaa' or noises to that effect. When it came to my turn I obliged with zest, and for the second time that afternoon speech forsook Miss Bassin.

'Once again!' she said after a disbelieving pause. And once again I thought I repeated what I thought I heard. Her lips pursed slightly but the gaze through the plate glass spectacles was more puzzled than unkind. She hit one note at one end of the keyboard and then one at the other end.

'Can you hear any difference?'

Of course I could hear a difference between a *ding* and a *dong* and I told her so. She muttered something to the effect that that was some small consolation, but she suggested that I might like to sit in one of the seats at the far end of the class-room till the end of the lesson and, perhaps, read a book till she was ready to give me some undivided attention. It was mortifying, but there was nothing else for it but to sit in solitary silence while the rest of my friends received their first lesson in their own native music from someone who turned out, on later acquaintance, to be a White Russian.

At the end of the lesson, and for several weeks thereafter, I was afforded varying periods of what was elegantly described as 'private tuition' after the rest of the school had gone home, but even the indomitable Ethel Bassin had to confess defeat. She assured me, rather hesitatingly, that there wasn't much wrong with my ear. By which she meant, I suspect, that I could hear. She was to return to the fray in later years, but for the duration of her weekly visits thereafter I was dismissed to my small corner with a book, to the possible benefit of my English and the undoubted detriment of my ego.

For a couple of weeks I was able to cajole or bribe my young brother into keeping quiet about my ostracism, and questions about my musical prowess were side-stepped with relative ease. It was only when Miss Bassin began to dish out homework that it became impossible to maintain what was a pretence rather than a deception.

'Why don't you ask your brother to help you?' said my mother, having finally grasped that her younger son's query anent crochets was to do with music and not with knitting. As

44

luck would have it diplomatic relations between him and me were strained for some reason or other.

'He can't help me. Miss Casan says he's just a stookie at music; he's not allowed . . .'

'Miss *who*?' My father erupted from behind his *Daily Express*. 'Don't let me ever hear you making fun of a human failing or I'll take your trousers down and you won't be able to sit for a week!'

I seized on a chance to change the subject, making a mental note to get equal with my brother later.

'Why is it wrong to call her Miss Casan when you yourself call Duncan MacLennan "Deaf Duncan" and you call Mary Stewart "Lame Mary" because she limps and you call . . .'

'Will you keep quiet! Nobody asked you for your opinion!'

It was an old scenario, and one that is enacted between fathers and adolescent sons the world over. For most of the time we were very close friends and he rather welcomed it when I challenged his views in a genuine quest for knowledge, but when he suspected that I was being deliberately provocative he was liable to flare into a momentary rage. And doubly liable if he suspected that he wasn't on very secure ground.

'Those are our own people,' he said. 'It's different with somebody who comes among us as a stranger – and a lady at that.'

I was going to challenge the validity of his argument when my mother stepped in.

'Stop arguing with your father! And what's this about you being told you're a stookie at singing?'

'She never said . . .'

But my young brother was exultant at my humiliation and the whole story came tumbling out, with a graphic description of my exclusion from the nest of singing birds, and it was all I could do to prove that I hadn't practised a deliberate deception by not having admitted to it earlier. My mother was mortified beyond all normal reason. I don't know whether she had cherished a secret notion of a budding Caruso in the family or whether she expected her first born to excel in everything remotely connected with school and education. But there was no denying her disappointment, and her upbraiding had the effect of bringing my father round to my support.

'Well, if the boy can't sing, he can't sing,' he said. 'It's not as if he can't get through life without it.'

'So long as he keeps quiet on Sunday!' she said.

Sunday! I'd forgotten about that. Sunday was going to be the day of the christening, and already there was an undertow of excitement in the village, as there always was in anticipation of anything which savoured of a social event – be it cattle sale or wedding. We had a family stake in this particular event because the infant to be christened was the little girl who had been born to James and my cousin Mary nine months and a few days after their wedding (the exactitude of the period had been checked and double checked by the women of the village with much counting of fingers, and had caused them to concede that there might be some efficacy in a mainland honeymoon after all). At the time, the idea of a honeymoon away from the island had been slightly sneered at as 'swank' and Great Aunt Rachel had been heard to declare that the morning after her wedding she had been up at dawn to milk the minister's cows at seven o'clock as usual, and that 'the young folk of nowadays couldn't even survive their first bedding without a convalescence'.

Just as the wedding of James and Mary had been the first wedding in the new village, so the christening of Jane was to be the first christening. Jane was not the first child to be born in the village – not by any means – but, at that time, the Presbyterian Church in Scotland was emerging from one of its many upheavals and our parish hadn't decided whether it was going to go out on a limb of fundamentalism or going to return to the arms of the 'Big Church' as the mother 'Church of Scotland' was called. Consequently our local pulpit was untenanted for a long period and our more urgent spiritual needs were attended to by divines from here, there, and everywhere. Christening, for some reason or other, didn't seem to rate high on the calendar of priorities and, during the years of ecumenical uncertainty, the new arrivals were being stock-piled, unchristened, like automobile chassis awaiting engines during a period of strike.

46

James and Mary couldn't afford to join the queue. He had gone off to the Merchant Navy shortly after his marriage and it was by sheer good luck that the end of his first voyage coincided with the birth of his first child. Nowadays, seamen are flown home from the ends of the earth by Concorde if Granny develops a verucca but, in those days, it was a man's bad luck if a crisis of any kind hit his family when he happened to be on the wrong side of the world. For all anybody knew, James's next trip might last for a couple of years and so it was decided to get the christening over during his three weeks of leave. At the root of it also, I suspect, was the islander's traditional and lingering distrust of the sea and the feeling that the end of the next voyage must not be taken for granted. Anyway, it was decided that a minister from a neighbouring parish should be enlisted to perform the ceremony on the afternoon of the last Sunday of James's leave, and – since it hadn't been decided which hallowed path of sectarianism our congregation was going to follow – the christening was going to be celebrated in the house.

James and Mary had set the community by the ears when they let it be known that the infant was going to be called Jane. There wasn't anything wrong with the name as such. It wasn't unknown; it appeared, respectably, in the newspapers from time to time. But it wasn't a family name; it wasn't even a village name. For generations past our people had called their first-born after the wife's mother or the husband's father (depending, naturally enough, on whether the child was female or male!) and from then on succeeding infants were given family names from alternating sides of the pedigree – moving into the realms of uncles and aunts only after the four grandparents had been commemorated. The system hiccuped slightly from time to time: for example if three girls arrived in succession then the third one was destined to go through life burdened with an adaptation of a Grandfather's name and, even now, when exotic names like Samantha and Clarinda are beginning to creep into the occasional lineage, it isn't unusual to encounter a wisp of a Hebridean girl bowed under an uncompromising name like Hectorina or Martinetta – signalling that the girl is the third of three females and that, lurking somewhere, there was a grandfather craving a whiff of immortality. Perhaps it wasn't even the name of Jane that caused the mild stushie in the village, but the reason for it which was, quite simply, that James had once sailed as a deckhand on a ship called *The Lady Jane*. Somebody with a tongue that could 'clip cloots', as they say, was quick to point out to Mary that she was fortunate her own father hadn't been given to fancy notions because he had sailed for years on a yacht called *The Yamahurra*!

But if the advent of the christening caused a stir in the village it caused dismay in the school when the teacher announced that the last hour of Friday afternoon (an hour normally regarded as a leisure period) would be devoted to the *Shorter Catechism*, and, in particular to Questions 94 and 95 which we had not yet reached in the course of our normal morning sessions of religious instruction. Questions 94 and 95 were (and are) respectively *What is baptism?* and *To whom is baptism to be administered?* And the answers are very complicated indeed. Question 95, in particular, takes a typically Presbyterian approach by responding in the negative: *Baptism is not to be administered to any that are out of the visible church, till they profess their faith in Christ and their obedience to him; but the infants of such as are members of the visible church are to be baptized.* We were instructed to get our parents to help us over the weekend, and to come back to school on Monday with our responses word perfect.

I spent the Friday night crouched over the little book of many words, going on the principle that it was better to get the grind over on the Friday night and leave the rest of the weekend free for play. My father was more exhausted than I was by the time the night was over, because to him fell the task of trying to explain all the obscure references in the texts, and though he was as bilingual as any father in the village he was hard put to it to find simple Gaelic interpretations of phrases like *doth signify and seal our ingrafting into Christ* and *members of the visible church*. When I pressed him for an example of an *in*visible church he remembered that he had the byre to secure for the night, and he left me with an assurance which was now becoming monotonous – 'that I would understand it all when

48

I grew up'. And so I abandoned any attempt at understanding and got down to the business of mugging the whole thing up word by word, feeling like a budding Rembrandt being made to paint by numbers. By Monday morning, like all my fellow sufferers, I was parrot perfect, and the teacher was mighty pleased.

Although no further reference had been made to the subject, my mother had obviously spent ten days agonizing over the revelation that I wasn't opera fodder, and, on the Saturday night while she was putting the finishing touches to a less garish pair of trousers that she had made for me she mentioned with studied casualness that there would be singing at the christening – two psalms, she thought.

'O good! Will they be ones I know?'

She winced, and agreed rather sorrowfully that they might be. 'But,' she said, 'you're not to sing.'

'Why not? Anybody can sing psalms; you just sing the line after the precentor. It's easy.'

'That's not the point. I want you to promise me that you'll keep quiet.'

Some instinct told me that this was a situation that could be exploited, and so I said nothing.

'Do you promise?'

'I don't know.'

For once in her life she resorted to bribery.

'Look here. I'll give you thruppence if you manage to keep quiet for the whole of the service. I'll give it to you on Monday morning, and you can spend it any way you like. Will you promise now?'

Of course I promised. Thruppence was a vast sum of money in my youthful world – enough to buy six bars of Toffee Cow in the Duchess's shop. I went to bed thinking that it was a strange thing – to be offered payment for *not* doing something.

Next day I felt very important indeed as I walked down the road with my parents. I was the only child in the village allowed to the christening; the others had had to be content with the little party which Mary and James had given on the Saturday afternoon – a new fangled idea which didn't meet with approval among the older folk because it smacked of mixing revelry with religion – but I was a relative of the new baby's and, besides, I was now what was termed 'a big boy'. Nevertheless, with the exception of the baby I was by far the youngest person present, and as we went through the door my mother seized a chance to pull me aside and reiterate her instructions on behaviour. . . . I was not to talk except when I was spoken to, and even then I was to give replies and *not* opinions; I was not to laugh at anything whether I thought it funny or not; and, above all, I was to observe strictly my contract not to sing. The last inhibition was the only one that irked me even though I stood to gain thruppence; whatever Miss Bassin might feel about my talents in the realms of secular singing I still felt it in my bones that I had a contribution to make to the psalms.

Everybody was there. All the relatives from Great Aunt Rachel downwards – seated stiffly on straight-backed chairs in a semi-circle round the room. The formal seating arrangement would have inhibited conversation even on a weekday, and the long silences were broken only by Aunt Rachel's normally timid husband who kept on sighing 'Aye, aye' to himself and rubbing the bald bit on the top of his head. James looked as if he had been starched into his navy blue serge suit; he looked flushed and uncomfortable, and every now and then he kept glancing furtively at a booklet which he kept slipping out of his breast pocket and which bore a strong resemblance to an aged copy of the *Shorter Catechism*. The only thing that broke the monotony for me was the discovery that when I slid up or down on my chair my new trousers remained where they were, like a snail's shell remaining still while its tenant slips in and out of it. I had a splendid game to myself, trying to calculate how far I could move without alerting the trousers, and I became so engrossed that I didn't even notice the big stern-looking minister entering the room. He, alone, looked totally at ease and, if anything, was tending towards the irreverent with his reference to the state of the crops and the peat and other worldly things. I came to the conclusion that, being on more intimate terms with the Lord than the rest of us, he had special dispensation to talk about such things on the Sabbath. However, he didn't waste much time on small talk and, after a few minutes, he asked Mary and James to step forward. They did so, with Jane by now sound asleep in her father's arms, blissfully unaware that he was trembling so much that it looked as if, at any moment, he would drop her.

There was a prayer and a reading from the Bible and then Murdo Mor precented a psalm in the singing of which everybody joined except me. It was one I knew well, and the temptation was sore, but I kept my lips tightly closed and thought of thruppence. The minister then intoned a little homily on the responsibilities of parenthood and, during each of several pauses, Mary nodded and James mumbled something as if on cue. When that was over, James was asked to hand the baby over to Mary and, from a certain stiffening on the part of the audience, I guessed that something important was going to happen. I got the shock of my life when the minister produced a copy of the *Shorter Catechism* and began to fire questions at a demoralized looking James.

What is the chief end of man?

James told him.

What rule hath God given to direct us how we may glorify and enjoy him?

James knew that one too. But as the inquisitor moved relentlessly on, picking questions at random, little beads of sweat began to break out on the upper lip of the man whom I had once heard boast that he had been drunk in every pub from Southampton to Singapore. However, he managed to navigate the treacherous waters of *the estate of sin and misery*; he steered his way round *effectual calling*; and he coped manfully with a random selection of the ten commandments. In short, in my opinion James was doing remarkably well for a man who had been away from school for a handful of years; but as the pages were turned relentlessly over it was becoming clear that he was becoming less and less sure of himself, and I began to suspect that his revision had become less thorough as he had waded through the first fourscore questions. He managed to convey that *faith in Jesus Christ* was indeed a saving grace; he gave a reasonable version of what *repentance unto life* ought to be; and then he fell at the water jump. 'Question Number 94,' said the minister, '*What is baptism?*' '*Baptism*' mumbled James

51

'is a sacrament . . .' and the minister nodded agreement. 'Wherein the washing with water in the name of the Father and the Son and the Holy Ghost . . .'. And having got over the water and the Trinity, James ran out of steam. There was a deathly, long silence which became harder and harder to bear. And then, as if from a distance, I hear my own voice, totally outwith my control, confidently, if squeakily, proclaiming '. . . doth signify and seal our ingrafting into Christ, and partaking of the benefits of the covenant of grace, and our engagement to be the Lord's.' I heard the voice finishing and I had time to notice that the minister was wide-eyed and open-mouthed, before by mother, crimson in the face, took me by the shoulder and led me from the room.

I recall nothing of her upbraiding. It was all lost on me when I realized that my thruppence was being forfeited. 'But I didn't sing!' I protested.

'You did worse,' she said. 'You made a fool of James and an even bigger fool of me!'

I suppose I did, in a kind of a way. But I don't think it mattered very much. Jane was duly christened, and now has children of her own who have both been perfunctorily splashed with dubious looking water purporting to have come from the River Jordan. Their father had to answer no questions from the Shorter Catechism. Nobody even raised an eyebrow when she called them 'Marigold' and 'Frederick Stephen'. And for sure these were never village names.

James called in to say Goodbye before he returned to sea, and he made soothing noises when my mother apologized for the embarrassment I had caused at the christening. 'Not at all,' he said. 'I would never have remembered that bloody covenant of grace bit if it hadn't been for our friend here, and that old codger of a minister might never have finished baptizing Jane.' I warmed at being referred to by James as 'his friend', and as I turned over his shilling in my pocket I thought that maybe it wasn't such a bad thing to be lacking in the gift of song.

Chapter Five

I grew up believing that Parliament was a nice, cosy, committee of gentlemen of faintly divergent beliefs who didn't really need a job but were glad of an extra £8 a week in those hard times. The impression of a friendly coterie was probably fostered by the fact that all the parliaments of my childhood were coalitions, and that my father (who maintained all his life that the ideal system of government for Britain was a Labour administration with a strong Tory opposition) voted socialist himself but at General Election times acted as the local agent for the Liberal candidate – because 'the poor man needed somebody to put up his posters for him and organize his meetings'. When it came to polling day he organized a Liberal car to take the allegedly infirm Liberal voters to the polling station five miles away in Leverburgh; Murdo Mor, who was a dedicated committee man with English every bit as good as my father's, laid on a car for the halt and the maim of the Labour party, and the Landlord, who had a car of his own, took the rest whom he assumed to be Tories. Since the community was reasonably young and fit the problem was always to find one aged member to sit in the front of each car to provide moral justification for its journey; but since it was generally conceded that our total votes were split evenly three ways it would have been as well for everybody to stay at home, by doing which they would have cancelled each other's votes out just as effectively. But Leverburgh was a stone's throw from the only hotel in the Southlands and opportunities for a day out were few and far between. The only elections which were really deemed to matter were the local County Council ones and, tragically for the fibre of the community, the choice there was between a selection of English-speaking incomers from the 'big houses' and a few ministers of the church with a genuine social conscience. The most hopeful development in the Western Isles in recent years, unknown then, is that local men of calibre have begun to take the reins of local administration into their own hands.

But there was increasing evidence that government at some level or other was beginning to take an interest in us. Once the new village had begun to take form and most of the new houses had been put up, the 'men from the ministries' had begun to tire of their tours of supervision and we were left to our own devices for a while. But then, when it was already almost too late, a new breed of official began to appear on the scene and hold meetings in the schoolhouse. Men and women with grittier mainland accents, well-worn suits and broken fingernails, who gave lantern-slide lectures on animal husbandry, land tillage and drainage, the use of fertilizers, milk and egg production and all the rest of it. Of these the 'Hen Wife' was far and away the most popular. She was young and attractive, with an infectious giggle, and men of all ages who had hitherto regarded hens as the curse of the cornfields began to accompany their wives to listen to lectures and see slides of Red Wynadottes and White Leghorns and Rhode Island Reds. I remember my mother being demurely flattered for being singled out as 'the woman who starves her hens in summer so that she can feed them up and get the eggs in winter'. It was a superb example of a woman with personality and charm being able to fire a sceptical audience with enthusiasm for a new expertise.

Already the old Highland malaise of 'what was good enough for my father and grandfather is good enough for me' was beginning to undermine the confidence of the community. Had those people come around at the beginning, when enthusiasm was high and before the world recession had begun to gnaw at us, the attitudes of mind might have been differently channelled and the future of the village differently moulded. There was a certain amount of sarcasm when a man from Barra was sent to teach weaving (what made a Barra man think he could teach Harris Tweed weaving in the island that had given the cloth its name?) but it was Peter Haggerty who planted in my father's mind the seeds of the idea of getting a loom of his own, and that loom was going to save us in the years ahead.

The agricultural experts had the most difficult time of it. Not only were they trying to change the established methods of ages, but they were too late. The man who addressed a packed schoolhouse and entertained us with his stories about the adventures of the potato on its travels from Peru to Europe in the sixteenth century was talking patent sense when he warned the crofters that their potato strains were running out, and that they must buy in some of the new seed being developed, but he was talking to men who couldn't now afford to invest in new seed potatoes: when he went away all that they remembered of his lecture was that the initial European resistance to the newfangled potato from South America had only been overcome when word got around that it was an aphrodisiac, and that it was the Empress Josephine's addiction to it which brought the great Napoleon to his knees with his heartfelt plea of 'Not tonight, Josephine!' That was good for a bawdy local joke or two, as the men opened up the last of the pits where the potatoes had been buried against the cold of winter and began to sift through the meagre remains of last year's crop for planting. 'Lay your seed potatoes out in a cool dark place for a few weeks till they're sprouting,' the man from the College of Agriculture had said. Fine theory, and fine for prosperous farmers with potatoes to spare. Our men would go cannily through their traditional *Kerr's Pinks* carefully cutting out the best 'eyes' from each potato for planting, keeping the rest of the tuber for the family pot. In normal times these left-over bits would be used as feed for the cattle, but these weren't normal times. Still, winter is long and spring is late in the islands, and the men of learning helped to pass the time.

Because spring was short it was hectic. The sea-wrack which the winter gales had left in long black smelly swathes on the beach had to be collected before the spring tides and the east winds cleaned it away again. Even the youngest members of the family were regimented to collect the stinking wrack into piles on the foreshore while the tide was out, and fathers and mothers crammed it into willow creels and carried it on their backs the half mile across the common grazing land to the crofts on the upper side of the road ready for spreading on the fields with manure from the byre to fertilize the land that was to be put under crops. It was back-breaking work, cold and wet and miserable, and I suppose not unlike the dreaded kelp collecting of such hated history. But we were doing it for our own benefit if not profit, and in time we would reap its harvest. Yet we knew we were working for a bare existence and, in the mind of the boy like myself, it was a further spur; a reminder that somewhere else there lay an easier life than this. Our parents told us so, our teacher told us so, and our books told us so; and all of them combined to convince us that the key to that better life was in books and learning. Had the authorities which had finally capitulated to the demands of the crofters for land of their own been whole hearted in their commitment, they would have sent their men from the colleges earlier to guide us, and they would have equipped us with even the rudiments of the mechanization which had already transformed the lives of small farmers on the mainland. We had been beguiled into a Garden of Eden without fruit trees, and without the means and the knowledge to make the fruit trees grow.

And yet spring was good. It brought alive again the camaraderie that had been dormant during the winter. When the peat-cutting started the families combined together to climb the hill and cut each others' peat banks in turn. The men who had ploughs and horses would turn the fields for those who hadn't. My own favourite was the big gentle quite-spoken man with the hole in his cheek, where a bullet had entered when he was 'going over the top' at Arras and had come out through his neck leaving him short of one tooth. When they found him he had enough blood left in him to keep him alive, and they were able to keep him so to see the rest of the war through. Like my own father and the others he never spoke about it, and I thought it was a big dimple till another boy told me what it really was. The best day of spring was the day on which he would arrive with his half Clydesdale horse and his plough and come in and tease my mother for a cup of tea till the rest of the village assembled.

My father and mother and I would have the field all spread

56

and ready with cow manure and seaweed a few days before, and we would be up early to lay out half a dozen bags of potato eyes at each end of the field, and as many buckets and basins as we could muster. In dribs and drabs the other crofters would arrive, some bringing their own hessian aprons made from old sacks, and a few of the women would come with covered baskets full of pancakes and oatcakes and home-made scones; one or two who had good yielding cows would arrive gingerly carrying pails of whey because, if the day was hot, the potato planting could be thirsty work and sore on the back into the bargain. The two or three venerable old women from the old township would trundle slowly along with their knitting; they were too old to help and nobody would expect them to; their presence was like a blessing, a routine which they had observed year in year out, and in their inmost ears they would probably be hearing the distant echo of the laughter which had been their own in days long past. I could see father's eyes glancing down the road and, though he never said anything, I knew that he was waiting for Great Aunt Rachel to arrive and that he would find some excuse to delay the proceedings till she did so. Not that excuses were hard to find. It took a long time to slice ropes of black twist tobacco with stubby cutty-knives, rub it between rough palms till the consistency was just right, scrape pipes and stuff them just tightly enough and no more, and then get them going and capped against the breeze. At last all would be ready. An experienced man would take the big black horse by the head and lead him in a straight line first up one side of the field and then down the other as the man with the hole in his cheek held the plough down, cutting the outer furrows which would mark the extent of our potato field for that year. After that the horse would follow the furrows on his own with only an occasional twitch on a rein to guide him as the ploughshare turned over the foot-wide sods with surgical precision. When the first gash was laid open several men with farmyard graips switched manure into it, and the rest, along with some of the women, followed – placing potato eyes at precise 18-inch intervals. Slowly, behind them, Great Aunt Rachel would walk with a mug of fresh water gently sprinkling each newly planted eye; nobody would pay any attention to her; nobody would speak;

the horse would be held still at the top end of the far-side furrow till she reached the end of the first one, whereupon she would straighten up and walk smartly down to the house shouting to my mother to bring the teapot to the boil. One or two of the men would smile to each other, and the man on the plough would crack his reins and the planting would get under way in earnest with its usual ribaldry and badinage and good humour. By some miracle of precision which I could never fathom there were never more than half a dozen potato eyes left over when the two ever widening sets of furrows met in the middle, and these were given to the horse while he was being unyoked.

It never occurred to me to ask anybody why Aunt Rachel performed her little ritual; there was something about the silence that hung over the field that discouraged curiosity. In any case the country boy grows up to accept traditional ritual as a matter of routine, and to probe that little ceremony would have been like asking my father what he said in his silent prayers when he 'took the Books' before bedtime. It was only a few years ago, when I was reading *Dr Salaman's History and Social Influence of the Potato*, that I read how – after the devastating Irish potato famine of 1845 – the Catholic priests in Ireland adopted the practice of sprinkling the newly-planted potatoes with Holy Water to bless the crop and ward off such tragedy again. In the Highlands, in that same year, we'd had our own potato famine of proportionately tragic dimensions; by then Great Aunt Rachel's forebears were already established as Clerics in the Presbyterian Church up on the hill, but in the Celtic countries rituals have had a habit of surviving in the folk tradition long after religious schisms and bigotry have obfuscated their original significance.

The potato planters sat down to a huge high tea when their day's work was over, swopping yarns and discussing the township's business. Never, as the starry-eyed writers of Hebridean romances would have one believe, quaffing drams and singing the night away into morning. I would fidget on the fringe of the gathering hopefully, till the man with the hole in his cheek would look up with a twinkle in his eye and say, 'I think the horse will be dry now, Finlay; would you like to do me a favour and take him home?' A favour! And the responsibility of it!

Time and the pretensions of sophistication have blunted many memories, but never the thrill of clinging on to the slippery bare back of a hefty plough horse pretending to be riding him like a cowboy from a story book while in reality the great beast was carefully picking his way home just as he would have done anyway. The man with the hole in his cheek had an understanding of boys surpassing that of anybody I ever knew, and in all our conversations he never spoke to me as if I were a year younger than himself. He never had a son of his own, but the last time I saw him he was surrounded with grandchildren and one of them was named after himself. Apart from the fact that he offered me a dram he spoke with me exactly as he did on the days of the potato planting.

It was shortly after the potato planting and the peat cutting were over that the first of our seasonal visitors arrived. The Black Man we called him; not in any pejorative sense, but because that's what he was. As yet we didn't have a name for him because he was a bird of passage, and he wasn't the same man every year. He was an Indian (the great sub-continent hadn't divided then) and it was one of the great mysteries how he and his fellows made their ways from wherever they came from across the Minch, and a greater mystery still how they expected to make their journey pay. But, shortly after the first cuckoo, the Black Man would appear with his heavy case strapped on to the carrier of his bicycle and knock politely on the door. Nobody ever turned anybody away so he was always invited in and offered a cup of tea which he always attempted to refuse. Visitors to the Outer Hebrides are subject to no hazards or dangers out of the ordinary save one. And that is tea. The seasoned traveller like myself, going back to my own native island, would be expected to cope with most of the traditional exigencies; but I have never found the art of dodging 'the wee cup of tea', which is anything but what it says. When the English say 'a cup of tea' they mean that; when the Hebridean hostess uses the same phrase it embodies at the very least two home-baked scones, two oatcakes with cheese and two pancakes! In the first house it is invariably welcome; in the second it is acceptable; in the third it is impossible, and equally impossible to avoid without giving offence. I have been driven to missing out visits to some of the homes of my best friends for fear of being killed with kindness, but I know not how Indian pedlars of those days survived when the acceptance of hospitality must have seemed a prerequisite if there was to be hope of a sale. But a sale there invariably was!

The procedure was always the same.

The housewife would say coyly and with patent sincerity, 'Now, it's very nice seeing you and I hope you will call back whenever you're passing this way, but I don't want you to be wasting your time opening your case. I don't really need anything today.'

'O no. Plenty time – just show you!'

'O, I know. Perhaps the next time you're passing.' Then, confidentially, 'To tell you the truth, times are very hard just now and I can't afford anything. You see, tweeds aren't selling just now and we just haven't got any money to spare.'

'Money very short everywhere. Very bad in Lewis. But fortunately it cost nothing to look.'

By now the case would be open, and the garment on top would be a dress of shimmering beauty and of total impracticability, but before the victim could say that, the Black Man would say it himself, 'This is no good. Too expensive. This is for the town, and a lady in Stornoway will buy it. But you feel.'

That was innocent enough, and honest. And irresistible. But there is something that happens to a woman when she feels a good quality material, that is like the break-down of the enzyme in the liver of the alcoholic. Layer after layer of garments of surpassing beauty (and rarity in a part of the world which then lived out of catalogues) would be folded neatly back on the flat lid of the case, with invitations to admire and feel but positive abjurations not to buy. In fact there was always a gentle undertone of suggestion that an offer to buy would be embarrassing because it would have to be turned down. And then a blouse would be flicked over rapidly without even an invitation to touch it. 'No good. Too like the one Mrs MacLaren bought.'

'Wait a minute. Let me have a look. Did Mrs MacLaren buy one of those?' (Strange, that. Mrs MacLaren hadn't sold a tweed in months either, and Charlie hadn't even sold a stirk at the last cattle sale.)

'No good for you. Too expensive. Right colour for Mrs MacLaren but wrong colour for you.'

It was probably the 'too expensive' suggestion that was the first twitch of the bait.

'It's very nice though. Can I have a look at it, please?'

'Sure. But not right. Mrs MacLaren more – er – more . . .' and the hands would indicate girth, while the tone bespoke reluctant delicacy.

'Stouter?'

'Yes. English not good. Mrs MacLaren more stouter.'

Two hits! Two palpable hits! Not only was this a man with good powers of observation, but here was a poor soul with poor English far from home.

The rest was easy. A blouse. A pair of knickers. Two pairs of pure silk stockings for the price of one pair, (The Trades Descriptions Act hadn't even been dreamt of) and, of course, it would indeed be sound policy to buy a light-weight semmit for the man of the house now that the warm weather was coming along. There would be just enough money in the shottle of the red kist, and the semmit would be produced first at the first appropriate time – maybe tonight, maybe tomorrow, but at the right time!

In truth, in our house the sale would be made even more easily if father happened to be in, because any visitor from across the Minch, far less from overseas, was a joy to him. The chance to exchange views with a stranger, the chance to hear news from foreign parts, the chance to open even a peep-hole on the outer world was bliss for him. For a gently extrovert man to feel that he was closed off forever in a small community, earning a livelihood in a manner for which for the greater part he had no heart, must have been a sorer trial than he admitted even to himself. Certainly he was shortly to take a step that would bring fresh interest into his life and build up an unexpected circle of friends, but he wasn't to know that then.

I don't know why the Black Man was accepted in the island without any of the appalling reactions that have met his kith and kin in more sophisticated communities. Or perhaps the answer lay in that very lack of sophistication. It may be that the man who lives close to the soil is more concerned with values deeper than the colour of skin. Perhaps we saw in him somebody who was struggling hard to survive as we were struggling ourselves. Certainly each one who came left behind him the sort of reputation that made his successor next year welcome, and, in due course, when one of them decided to settle in the community and marry into it, he was accepted and given a place of honour. But that was Ali, whom the older men called Alick as if he were one of themselves. It wasn't Ali who was alleged to have brought about the death of Hector MacGeachan's sharp-tongued sister; it was the man who sold Mrs MacLaren the blouse.

He earned every penny he pocketed, that man. Not only did he trundle our indifferent road of those days on his rackety old bicycle calling at every roadside house; he would get off his bike, prop it against the roadside fence and trudge up the winding footpaths to the remotest houses on the hillside, and he made his sales in the unpromising looking black houses as unerringly as he did in the croft house or the manse. It was just unfortunate that the young man he met on his way up the hill was one of the most popular rapscallions of the place, a lad in his late teens with a taste for the beer and an eye for the girls, but with a sense of humour that made him one of the most popular characters in the five villages, and would make a saint forgive him for sin. The story of the encounter was his own, told many times with a smile that was tinged with conscience.

'Ah, Mohammed. . .' he said.

'Excuse me my name not Mohammed. My name . . .'

'It doesn't matter; you're the man I'm looking for. See that house up there. That's Hector MacGeachan's house, and his sister wants to see you. She's out at the peat-bank just now but she'll be back home in a few minutes. The door's open and you're to go in and wait for her. She's desperate to see you; there's something she wants to buy for a wedding.'

The poor Black Man wasn't to know that there wasn't a wedding on the horizon in the whole island, and the idea of somebody actually so desperate to make a purchase that he mightn't even have to suffer yet another cup of tea must have been something beyond his wildest idea of success. And so –

thanking the cheerful messenger – he hoisted his case on his shoulder and climbed the steep track to Hector's house.

Now the description 'black house' doesn't mean very much to people who didn't know the pre-war islands, and to people in the Home Counties the totally appropriate alternative description of 'thatched cottage' conjures up a wholly inappropriate picture of a highly desirable, highly listed, National Trust type cottage with Norfolk reeds at the end of a Somerset lane. A 'black house' in the Hebridean sense (and Hector's was one of the last remaining ones in our parts) had a dry-stone wall about two feet thick, a roof of heather thatch, a floor consisting of the God's earth trampled solid by many generations, and a peat fire in the middle of the floor, with the smoke (or most of it) escaping through a hole in the roof – a hole which could not, of course, be directly above the fire or else the rain coming through would put the fire out. The window was deeply recessed and small. And all those qualities made for a house which could be very warm and comfortable but so dark that it earned to the full its description of 'black house'.

The Black Man would be no stranger to them. Up till the war they were still quite common in the Western Isles, before the islanders took the biggest leap forward in their history to the stone and lime 'white house' as the new type of building was, naturally, called for its very contrast.

The Black Man went into Hector's house and felt his way to a stool by the fire and sat and waited.

His informant hadn't been totally misleading. Hector's sister was indeed at the peat-bank, and about the time that the Black Man went into her house she was on her way back home with a small sack of peat which would keep her going till Old Hector got back from whichever house he was gossiping in, and, doubtless, she was framing the words with which to salute him when he got home. The poor woman flung down her sack, according to herself, and, gasping for breath from her exertions went into the house.

'Hello Miss MacGeachan,' said the voice.

Hector's sister nearly jumped out of her skin at the unexpected greeting. When she recovered sufficiently to peer into the darkness all she could see was a set of gleaming white teeth and a very large pair of disembodied white eyes staring at her from a height of three feet above the floor and she collapsed in a dead faint. So – nearly – did the Black Man. And the good Lord only knows what dire imaginings of punishment he dragged from his mental transposition of similar circumstances to whichever primitive part of the Raj he came from. He did what any man of any colour would be tempted to do. He picked up his case and ran for his bicycle.

When Hector MacGeachan got home, unaware that the Black Man had been in the country, far less of the circumstances, he fell over his virago sister, speechless for once, and prostrate on the floor. In falling he thrust out his hand to stop himself and put it right into the centre of the smouldering peat fire. It was his yell of pain as much as his collapse on top of her that brought her round out of her faint and, on Hector's own wistful admission later, her tonguing put the pain out of his hand for an hour. But it also brought out a forgotten spark of his manhood. He was prepared to accept much maligning for the sake of peace, but he was not going to accept the responsibility for two non-existent large white eyes and a set of smiling teeth in the dark. He was as superstitious as the next man, but that particular phenomenon didn't fit into any of the accepted catalogues of superstitions or premonitions. His sister was either hallucinating or lying, and he told her so in a voice that carried to the nearest house – which wasn't exactly next door.

Nobody ever heard where the Black Man whose name wasn't Mohammed disappeared to, but he was never seen in Harris again. Hector's sister survived for a week to harangue him and to stravaig the village telling her story, and a week was long enough for the village to be able to absolve everybody from guilt when she took a stroke and died.

'Poor woman,' they said. 'With that temper of hers it's a miracle that she didn't burst a blood vessel long since.'

Chapter Six

THERE is an old Gaelic proverb which says that 'no man ever saw his own tree plantation grow.' I'm sure that like most proverbs it has its equivalent in every language under the sun since all it's saying in effect is that subtle change and development are going on around us all the time, so gently that we don't notice them. I'm not sure that – in any language – the proverb is valid any more, because accelerating technology can change an area of our environment overnight; and as environments change so habits and modes of life change, and 'tradition' which we used to think of as the mellowing harvest of sown experiences, is now giving way to that thing known as 'a phase'. Distance and inaccessibility, and – above all – that stretch of ocean known as the Minch, allowed the Outer Hebrides to cling on to their old ways, good and bad, their language, and the depth of their religious belief, long after the power-houses of the cities had tended to send their waves of uniformity out over all but the remotest corners of the mainland. It's a generalization of course, because even cities cling on to their own enclaves of style and custom, and everybody knows that the great sprawl we call London is, basically, a huge collection of villages; but, in most of the everyday conducts of life, less and less separates the man in John O' Groats from the man at Land's End. The man in Barra watches the same *Coronation Street* as the man in Bermondsey; they watch the same politicians arguing the same points; and, inevitably, exposure to the same banalities and the same philosophies will produce common attitudes to most things.

The Minch has ceased to be a great dividing barrier between mainland Scotland and the Western Isles except in so far as the cost of crossing it puts a huge economic burden on the islanders. If it ceased to be an economic barrier and became a cultural one instead, then there might be a greater hope that the islands could survive to appreciate their own language, and the traditions which a language, more than anything else, encapsulates. But the airwaves and the airways don't acknowledge the sea as a hindrance, and both those have served to accelerate change in the islands more than anything else; the former because they overwhelm viewers and listeners with a beguiling and glossy alien culture; the latter because they have removed the mystique of time and distance for the very people who go in search of it. It is nice and convenient to have coffee at Heathrow and lunch in Harris, but one hasn't explored anything on the way. The airwaves had already begun to search us out by the time Hector MacGeachan lost his sister; the airways found us on the day they buried her.

There is no ultimate difference between the cold fact of death in Glasgow now and death in our village almost half a century ago, but there is a mighty big difference in the ceremonial attending it. When I go to a funeral in the city now I put my black tie in my pocket and wrap it round my neck in the crematorium car park, and I'll be taking it off again before the ashes have barely had time to cool, and hastening to vacate a parking space for a car in the next waiting cortège. When Maggie MacGeachan died, work in the village stopped for the three days of her lying, and for three nights men and women took it in turn to go and sit in 'the house of watching', a quiet, sober, and solemn version of what the Irish call a wake. There was none of the Irish festivity that playwrights have found so much inspiration from; just quiet talking about matters of life and, occasionally, a prayer from a man whose nearness to eternity gave him sufficient confidence and authority to pray. But during the three days there was much work to be done. Food had to be provided for those who came to pay their respects, and it turned out that Maggie (as people took to calling her now that her back was turned forever) had many relatives in the Eastlands who had found the distance too long to visit her while she was alive; the old women who, wise in the ways of birth and death, had to wash and lay her out; the men who had to go to the joiner three villages away and tell him to bring down the boards which he always had seasoning in the rafters of his workshop against the day that would require a coffin. Not that Old Hector's sister would require many boards; what there was of her in life was mostly tongue they used to say, but of course she had good points too, they were now remembering. When the morning of the day came, the joiner would deliver the coffin in good time along with a handful of screwnails.

Many island schools would close for the day, or at least for the afternoon of a funeral, but our school was only a quarter of a mile from the cemetery which served most of the island and if we closed for every funeral dozens of attendance days would be lost. So a respectful compromise was reached. The school closed for the whole day if a funeral concerned the immediate family of one of the 'scholars' as we were called, but if it didn't we merely stood in silence for a few minutes as a cortège passed the school; or, if it came from the opposite direction, we observed the silence for a token while during the period when the teacher adjudged that the graveyard service was being conducted. The latter ordinance would, in the normal course of events, have been observed for the Mac-Geachan funeral, but events did not turn out to be normal.

Ours was a one-teacher school, and, therefore, it was impossible for her to organize any form of segregated school activity, so 'drill' – or physical training – was tailored to exercises that the boys and girls could perform together without embarrassment to the latter. Gardening and cookery provided no problem at all; the boys took cookery along with the girls, and the girls were introduced to the skills of gardening along with the boys. The funeral was due to take place on a gardening afternoon – a fact which I could not possibly have remembered if the day hadn't turned out to be momentous; but not only do I remember what we were doing, I remember that it was an exceptionally beautiful afternoon. Gardening was very good fun. I have never been able to understand why the crofters were so indifferent to the possibilities of a vegetable plot unless it was because the depredations of the rabbits took the heart out of them. Certainly in our minute little school patch of light sandy soil we could grow vegetables of all ordinary variety – lettuce, turnip, beetroot and so on – and we were each able to take at least a token sample home from time to time. We did, on second thoughts, have the advantage of a plot surrounded by a high stone wall, to which the only access was through the school – and it would have been a fairly courageous rabbit who negotiated that.

We were all bent over our individual areas of horticulture, with the teacher sitting relaxed with a magazine which, we were lead to believe although it was never expressly stated, contained gardening notes. The fact that the cover proclaimed that it contained a revealing article about the present life and whereabouts of the Duke and Duchess of Windsor one week, and promised full coverage of the Royal State Visit of King George VI and Queen Elizabeth to Edinburgh next week, was probably coincidence. We weren't worrying anyway. Gardening was interesting, and we were allowed to talk quietly to each other while we were getting on with our work. And then we heard a car approaching and we straightened up of one accord.

'Never mind the car. Get on with your work or I'll take you all inside and give you sums!'

We knew perfectly well she didn't mean it, just as we knew she'd be having a sly look herself when the car came nearer – because one could glean a lot of contemporary social history from the purposeful to-ings and fro-ings of cars in those days.

'It will be a car for the funeral,' I whispered to Jamie MacInnes who was weeding the row beside me. 'I heard my mother saying that Hector MacGeachan had relatives in Tarbert.'

'Shut up,' he hissed. 'I think she's forgotten about the funeral, and if she remembers she'll take us inside to stand up!'

I couldn't quite see the logic of going inside in order to stand up for the mandatory minutes of silence, when the people most closely involved would be performing their obsequies by the graveside in the open air. I didn't argue with him because

68

Jamie was a bright lad and he could read the teacher's mind better than any of us. But there was one thing he didn't jalouse, just like the rest of us; and that was that this was no approaching car. As the droning noise kept getting nearer there was no suggestion of the noise of tyres on gravel, and suddenly somebody yelled, 'It's an aeroplane!' and even the teacher sprang to her feet.

Aeroplanes weren't totally new to us. On very rare occasions we had heard them overhead, and had even seen the odd one like a dot in the sky in the distance. But never one as low as this. It was coming over the Back of Scarista Hill, a grey bi-plane moving incredibly slowly – it seemed to us as we stared open-mouthed at it – and it kept losing height as it approached, till by the time it was overhead we could read the letters printed on its side, and, as he passed, the pilot waving to us.

'It's going to crash!' somebody shouted.

'Nonsense!' the teacher yelled, 'Didn't you see the pilot waving; he wouldn't be doing that if he was going to crash, would he?' And then, after a pause, and without the slightest attempt to keep the excitement out of her voice, 'But it's going to land on the sands, that's what! Listen to me. You can all run down to see it, but then come straight back here and tell me all about it. Remember now, straight back. Off you go!'

We went like 13 greyhounds out of their traps, racing down the machair land and the rolling dunes that lay between us and the flat tidal sands of Northton. We were to realize later that our own expansive beach was too soft and yielding for an aeroplane to land on, whereas the sands of Northton are as hard as a blaes tennis court – when the tide is out and they're baked in the sun. I don't suppose the two miles of machair between Scarista and Northton have ever been covered in faster time, and, sure enough – when we arrived – there, like a grotesque double-winged fulmar, the grey aeroplane was resting on the sands with its propeller idling to a stop and the pilot climbing down out of his cockpit. As we arrived we were aware of people converging on the scene from every direction, from Northton village, from Kintulavig further down the road, from our own village, and down from the moor's edge – looking like people from another world – an incongruous knot of people in black with the men wearing black ties.

When the excitement had begun to die down, one of the older girls passed word round that the teacher was expecting us back, and she pointed out that it had been good of her to let us free. 'Remember Miss Dalbeith?' she said. 'She'd have locked us indoors and not let us even *see* the aeroplane!'

'The aeroplane wouldn't have come if that bitch was here!' one of the boys muttered as we headed back for school. Those of us who remembered Miss Dalbeith were, mercifully, getting fewer; the generations were rolling on.

'I bet you she'll give us an essay about the aeroplane,' Jamie said as we jogged along.

'No,' I said. 'That would just be giving herself work correcting them.'

'Like buggery,' Gillespie puffed. 'She'll give us a composition and then not bother reading it. Anything to keep us in the house in the evening.'

In fact, quite perceptibly, our noses were being eased more and more towards the grindstone. There was a definite firming of work and of purpose, and we all knew that it was because the bursary examinations were drawing near. The generation immediately ahead of the three of us would, in fact, be sitting the County examinations and having their futures decided in a few weeks' time, and then next year it would be our turn. When we got back to school, it turned out that Jamie and Gillespie were half right and that I was totally wrong. The schoolroom looked as dark as a winter's evening after the sunshine on the white sands, and as dull as a moorland cavern. From where I sat I couldn't see the teacher's face as she stood silhouetted against the window questioning us on what we had done and what we had seen, nor could I get a word in edgeways for the girls and the infants blattering on and on – the girls about the pilot and the infants about the aeroplane. At last she called a halt to the hubbub.

'Now listen all of you,' she said at last, and Gillespie nudged me hard in the ribs. 'I've been thinking while you've been away. You've had a marvellous experience, and by the time you're grown up you'll be travelling in aeroplanes as people now travel in buses. I want the two top classes (we'll let the young ones off this time) . . . I want the two top classes to go home and write a one page composition – just one page – describing exactly what happened today, what you saw and what you thought about it. Remember now – not just a description of the aeroplane but a description of the whole scene – and then tomorrow I'll pick the best bits out of all the essays and I'll send the story off to the *Daily Record*. Who knows? One of you might work on a newspaper one day, and you'll look back on this as your starting point. Right. Here are your papers, and off you go!' As we filed past her she handed the members of the two oldest classes foolscap pages with our individual names already written across the top.

'I told you so,' somebody muttered as we went through the school gate. But nobody really condemned the idea. The *Daily Record* (a Kemsley paper) was then challenging the monopoly of Beaverbrook's *Express*, and cartoon strips like *Lauder, Willis and Lorne* (founded on the three leading Scottish Music Hall figures of the time) and *Bringing up Father* were attacking the empire of *Rupert Bear*, but I doubt if either Press Baron was filling his coffers appreciably in Scaristavore. Newspapers were not peaking much circulation in our village although the occasional ones that we saw were fat, and beginning to breathe optimism.

'She forgot the Lord's Prayer,' somebody said when we were well clear of the school. And, sure enough, for the only time that I could remember the teacher had forgotten to close the day in the usual way.

'Shut up or she'll call us back if she hears you.'

My father still hadn't returned from the funeral when we got home, and my mother was not in the best of form as she scrubbed the flabby ware potatoes for our evening meal.

'I've never heard the like of it,' she said. 'People rushing away from a funeral to go risking their necks in an aeroplane.'

'There hasn't been an aeroplane before!' My brother had begun to practise the art of retort, and he hadn't yet learnt when it was wiser to keep quiet. My mother wasn't a deeply religious woman in any of the fashionable fanatical moulds,

71

but she had a wholesome respect, not untinged with superstition where matters of death were concerned.

'You keep quiet and bring in two pails of water from the burn.'

'I can't carry two pails.'

'You can carry one pail at a time, and if they're not full to brim when I look at them you'll get the fetter-rope across your calves!'

She really was in a bad mood, and I didn't even chance a smirk in my brother's disgruntled direction. The fetter rope was the short rope that she used to tie round the cows' hind legs when she was milking, and it always hung on a nail beside the mantelpiece, not because she was sadistically keen on wielding it – although it was a favourite grudge of hers that she was always being cast in the role of dispenser of punishment; the fetter rope was there so that she would know exactly where to lay hands on it at milking times. But it was a deterrent, in those days before the word had assumed any more awful significance.

My father came in whistling cheerfully just as the salt herring were coming to the boil, pulling off his black tie as he came through the door.

'Dinner's ready!'

'God look down on you woman, you don't expect me to sit down to potatoes and herring in my Sunday suit, although I confess I'm starving.'

'You didn't have any qualms about going chasing off after an aeroplane in your Sunday suit and your funeral tie, from what I hear. A judgment will come on you people for your behaviour today. Mrs MacRae was in here and she'd been watching the whole thing from the Back of Scarista Hill. She said that you looked for all the world like a stream of black cockroaches making for a dead sheep's carcase. It was easy to see that it was the missionary and not the minister conducting the funeral service, Mrs MacRae was saying, or he wouldn't have tolerated the gang of you rushing off to an aeroplane before poor Maggie MacGeachan's soul had been laid to rest. Mrs MacRae was horrified, and I'm not surprised!'

'If God sends an aeroplane for Hetty MacRae's soul the way he did for Maggie's *I'll* be the one who's surprised!'

'John!'

My father also knew when to shut up, but gave us a broad wink as he went through to the other room to change. . . .

Our report was published in the *Daily Record* the following Saturday – a distillation, as Miss Martin had promised, of all the best efforts submitted to her the next day. Alas, it contained not one single word that I had contributed; I had gone off on a very oblique new angle (inspired by stories of the use of aircraft in the Great War) about aeroplanes with machine guns some day threatening Northton Sands. I searched out the story just a few days ago with some considerable help from the Mitchell Library in Glasgow, and I can do no better than quote it verbatim – in the certain knowledge that the *Daily Record* will not mind after all this time. It was headed:

FIRST AEROPLANE IN HARRIS

With a whirr of sand rising from its landing place and settling in its wake, an aeroplane made a landing in Harris, on the golden Northton sands. Soon nothing was to be heard but the patter of little feet and big feet, racing cyclists, hooting cars, all forgetful of speed limits, making for that unique object, the first aeroplane to land in Harris. What a scene of animation and what a babel of voices! Countless questions were showered on the patient pilot who imparted the required information, allowed the spectators to examine the machine and offered them a short and free trip in the air.

With a full complement of local people from Scarista and Northton, the 'plane rose gracefully, sped across the sands rising higher and higher and in ever widening circles, thrilling the passengers and causing the panic-struck cattle and horses to scatter hither and thither.

The islands of Taransay, St Kilda, Shellay, Pabbay, Bernera, Killegray, Ensay were seen in rapid succession ere the delighted and grateful passengers were disembarked on the sands.

73

A third landing was effected on a neighbouring meadow, which is evidently an ideal landing place.

The initials are MM. But I remember that the gist of the story was Jamie MacInnes's, already displaying the beginnings of a talent which, alas, the scourge of the Hebrides at the time did not allow to flower. One phrase, though, was certainly inserted by the schoolteacher who'd been to college on the mainland: to this day 'speed limits' are unheard of in the Western Isles – except for one in Stornoway, whose introduction had as its one result, according to one Lewisman, that 'the Harris bus had to accelerate'.

As I thumbed through that old *Daily Record* I stumbled across bits and pieces that blew ashes off the embers of memory. Some anniversary of the days of Savoy Hill was being celebrated by the BBC, although the wireless had not yet reached our village. Not quite. But it and the aeroplane came in the year that Maggie MacGeachan died, and between them they heralded the beginning of the great levelling out which is now accelerating around us, and bringing Heathrow ever nearer to Harris, and Bermondsey to Barra.

Chapter Seven

T HAT summer was supposed to be my last holiday in the Northlands anyway, and as things turned out it was just as well that everybody had become conditioned to the idea. It saved my Big Grandfather the embarrassment of having to declare me *persona non grata*, thus hurting the feelings of his younger and favourite daughter; and it saved giving the neighbours a chance to detect a rift in the family lute. From the time that we had left the Northlands and settled in the new village in the south, I had travelled north every summer and spent the long school summer holidays with Big Grandfather – a near neighbour of Wee Grandfather, my father's father. Thus I was encouraged to maintain the strong family bonds which were so treasured in the Hebrides, and which were more difficult to maintain in the case of ourselves once we had uprooted ourselves to become strangers in a strange land. I suspect that, family feeling altogether apart, my mother was keen that I should have some fragmentary roots in the Northlands because, much as she liked the freedom of her own home in an undeniably beautiful setting, she missed the community closeness in which she had been brought up – a closeness which was really the product of overcrowding, and part of the very reason why it had become necessary for our people to move and follow their star to the good land and the wide open spaces of the south. But the open spaces can be daunting to the person not born to them, and the unease my mother suffered from was not so very different from that affecting overcrowded city dwellers finding themselves transplanted to planners' paradises. And, as far as I was concerned, not only did I have an indefinable soul link with the Northlands – much as I loved the freedom of the machair – but I was experiencing the holiday syndrome of the country boy coming to town.

The Northlands had a town in the shape of Tarbert with 13 shops, a pier which bustled thrice a week when the ship came in, a harbour which swarmed with fishing boats in those days, and a surpassingly beautiful anchorage which was speckled white in summer with rich men's yachts. And the country had an awesome beauty of its own; a land of great grey slabs of Lewisian gneiss dominating the heather, sprinkled with trout lochs that sparkled in the evening sun like unexpected diamante on a cloak of hodden grey. There was freedom too; the kind of freedom that grandparents lavished on their young guests before grandads became golfers and grandmothers took to bingo and cocktail bars. There was another freedom for me in the shape of a big house with an upstairs and a room to myself; a room with coom ceilings and a skylight which I could open on the morning to watch the Scalpay fishing boats chugging in leisurely through the yachts with their choruses of seagulls that seemed to be attached to them like wind-blown veils. And there was new company; a host of cousins above all else, including one of my own name who was a year or two older than me and wiser than me in the ways of the adolescent world. He was the only person who was dearer to my heart than Gillespie, because he knew a thing or two, and what he didn't know he invented. He taught me to smoke and when the day of reckoning came it was he who paid the price much much too soon.

Sixteen miles of a remove doesn't sound like much of an adventure for a holiday, but the miles are as long as the state of the road. The first little bus that attempted to establish a weekly connection between north and south was a 7 seater which took an hour to do the journey, and the men had to get out and push it up the steeper hills. The next bus was bigger and posher and it must have had its origins in some greater part of the mainland, perhaps the city, because it had a notice saying 'Spitting forbidden' – which was good for a laugh among men who smoked black twist and bogey roll. The concession to run the first thrice-weekly service was won by the man with the 'new' bus or, rather, *accepted* by him because everybody was sure it would never pay, and nobody could decide who was dafter – the man, who had saved up five pounds of his own money, or the banker who had lent him another five to pay for the bus. But the man had a personality that would have taken him to the top in any walk of life. His boast was that he had attended school for only two days and for them only because his grey-bearded grandfather had sat in the classroom with him to make sure he didn't run away. He hid an extraordinary shrewdness behind a beguiling eccentricity and the people who laughed at him were the people who loved him most. Many years later, when the bus with the 'Spitting forbidden' sign had multiplied into a large fleet – which, on the mainland, would have been a target for takeover – I teased him about his wealth and, over a dram, asked him what he reckoned he would have achieved if he had stayed in school and acquired an education. He replied with beguiling simplicity, 'I'll tell you that, boy; I'd be a bloody schoolmaster.' But that was long after the days of the last holiday, far less the first!

Invariably I set off for the Northlands the day after school closed for the summer holidays at the beginning of July, and without fail I landed at Big Grandfather's the week before summer Communion. I always arrived with money in my pocket because the man with the bus had a very bad memory when it came to accepting fares from little boys, and he would swear that he had been paid at the beginning of the trip. By the time Communion was over I was rich beyond measure.

Communion means to the city man a holy ritual at a morning service, three or four times a year if he's a Scottish Presbyterian; oftener if he belongs to one of the other faiths. But Communion in the Hebrides was a festival in those days. It began with us on Thursday, which was a Fast Day, although it was marked only by the cessation of all activity and the closing of all shops rather than by the ancient act of starving. People would assemble from the far corners of the islands, starting to arrive on the Wednesday evening having walked sometimes 20 miles. They would arrive in their hundreds and

77

find accommodation with friends in the village in which the ceremony was due to be held, and from the Thursday to the Monday they would attend two church services a day and a series of evening prayer meetings as well, before the more devout of them moved on to a similar festival in another village or maybe another island. It was a moving and sometimes overwhelming experience to be caught up in the tension and occasional hysteria which could develop; it was an unforgettable new experience for me, since our own parish didn't have a resident minister at the time and consequently the ritual of twice-yearly communion had gone into abeyance. It was a strange beginning to the holiday, having to be on best behaviour for five days of continuous worship, and I got the full brunt of it in Big Grandfather's house because, although he wasn't an especially devout man himself, he had plenty of accommodation to offer and he was very hospitable.

For the days of Communion time I had to surrender my little attic room and sleep in whichever corner was available, because, with anything up to 20 guests in the house, bedspace was at a premium. But it was worth it. Each guest who arrived was, by virtue of being of Christian spirit, also disposed to be of Christian charity and every handshake for a little boy was accompanied by a surreptitious sixpence or a shilling – or even a half-crown, if the visitor happened to be a comfortable merchant haunted by the thought of that camel and the eye of the needle. In early years I still had money left to take back home with me at the end of the holiday, but when my cousin had taught me to smoke I found my donations weighing less heavily on my pocket.

And as I got older I became less amenable to the disciplines of Communion time and instead of allowing myself to be led by the hand to endless church services I found ways of slipping off unnoticed and spending the day trout fishing with the other Finlay. All of this was part of the rebelliousness of puberty which, strangely enough, led to more tension between Big Grandfather and myself than, as is more traditionally the case, between my father and myself. The difficulties were exacerbated by the fact that it was undoubtedly from Big Grandfather that my mother had developed her nervousness and the imagination to conjure up the possibilities of danger in connection with the most ordinary of boyish ploys. My grandfather, of course, had the added responsibility of looking after somebody else's child and he would never have forgiven himself if some mishap had befallen me while I was in his charge for what must have felt to him sometimes as seven very long weeks. He saw danger everywhere. On the shore cliffs below the house, in the tarns on the moor where my cousin and I used to wander, in the deep river pools where we fished brown trout, and even in the tinker camps which sprang up along the road which led between the houses of my two grandfathers.

The tinkers certainly looked a fearful lot. Big black avised men who got drunk even on Communion Saturdays and who fought with each other, and would have fought even with the visiting ministers if they had crossed their paths. Their women were large-boned and black-eyed, and they could be whining and suppliant when they chose or aggressive and foul-mouthed if they were crossed. They made their living out of selling odds and ends of ironmongery, mending pots and pans and making tin milk pails. They were extremely proud and tribal and regarded themselves as descendants of the broken clans who had not been cowed by the harsh Hanoverian repressions which followed Culloden, and rather despised the rest of us because we had succumbed to the soft life and good manners. Their marriages and their funerals were conducted according to age-old secret customs of their own, and they married not only within their own tribes but within their own sects, which had their individually defined traditions and taboos. God help the ordinary man who, in a drunken moment, made a pass at a tinker lassie; he was liable to end up in a ditch with every bone in his body broken and no trace or evidence of who did it. But nobody ever got so drunk as to try. I passed their encampments day in day out, and all I ever got was grunted Gaelic greeting in an accent that was different from our own. Tinkers, like Holy Communion attenders, had special standards for youngsters, and I could never understand Big Grandfather's hatred of them.

It was with my cousin that I got to know the Northlands like the palm of my hand. He knew every trout loch, and he had an instinct which told him unerringly when it was safe to go on a landlord's privately stocked loch in search of Loch Leven trout – instead of the pink-fleshed brown trout of the mountain streams. Our only equipment was a willow rod with a simple line and hook on it, but he could thread a worm so that it looked as live and juicy and wriggly as when he yanked it out from beneath its cowpat or its stone. And if he didn't have a line and hook it didn't bother him unduly. He could see a trout below a stone where I could see nothing but slippery pebbles and peaty mud; and he could slide up to the bank on his belly without causing the ground to tremor, and tickle the trout till it opened its gills with pleasure so that he could slip his finger in and howk it on to the heather with one flashing movement of his forearm. I could never master the art. 'It's just like a girl,' he would say as he lay back flushed with success beside a big brown trout flapping on the heather. 'You just keep stroking in the right places till the right moment comes and she opens up for you, and once you get your finger in there the rest's just a matter of moving in on your advantage. And man, oh man . . .' He was a Lothario by his way of it, with a power of description that set my head and my belly on fire just listening to him.

During those later summer holidays we became like blood brothers and he used to look forward to the day when I would win my bursary, as he was sure I would do, and come to Tarbert School. What ploys we would have then! What fun there was in Tarbert village on a winter's night, which, of course, I had never experienced – nor would ever have been allowed to, at that age, by Grandfather. The temptations to work hard to win the bursary were fast becoming stronger than mere scholastic ambitions, and I began to see Junior Secondary School as a brave new era even although I would, perforce, be a lodger in Big Grandfather's house. That had always been understood from the beginning. The £11 of bursary which I hoped to win would barely cover the better clothes that I would require for Tarbert School and a minimal contribution to my grandmother for my keep. Without that bursary I would never graduate to Tarbert, and the more I talked to my cousin the more alluring Tarbert sounded. Yes, this would have to be my last holiday; the next time I came it would be to stay, and the return to the village between terms would be the holiday then.

My cousin, with no malice aforethought, helped considerably towards making that last holiday short.

'Have you got the usual load of holy Willies and praying Marys in your Big Grandfather's?' he asked on Communion Saturday.

'Yes.'

'And are you sleeping in the cubby-hole as usual with two Lewis crones in your own bed?'

That was a sore point, and he knew it. I treasured more than anything else the privacy of that little attic room with the coom ceilings and the skylights.

'Well Sandy Malcolm was telling me a trick that he heard at the salmon fishing in Perthshire, and it'll get you the laugh of your life – and I'll bet you two pounds to your Communion takings that they won't be back next year!'

He knew that my little gifts from the Communion visitors had amounted to just under two pounds, which was a small fortune, and he knew that I knew he didn't have two *shillings*; but that was just his way of being emphatic, and he would have given me his last penny, far less take a halfpenny from me. He proceeded to detail the joke that Sandy Malcolm had brought back from the Tay fishings, and by the time he was finished I was sobbing with laughter.

'It can't fail man. And there's no way you can be caught unless you play daft. I'd give my last fag to be there to see it; make sure you remember every word that's said so that you can tell me.' He sent me off with two Woodbines to smoke on the way home. 'Keep your eye open for the new maid in the doctor's house,' he whispered as I was going away. 'She's from Skye with red hair and tits like turnips, and the Tarbert boys say she's game. Have a look round church tomorrow.'

I set off into the night with that irritating tingle in my lower belly again, and the tin he had given me tucked carefully below my ganzie. 'Red hair and tits like turnips.' There wouldn't be many to fit that description in church on Com-

munion Sunday. It was dark by the time I was nearing the
tinkers' encampment, and I could hear it long before I came
in sight of it round the Devil's Elbow as the hairpin bend in
the road was called. When I did see it, it was like a battlefield
such as one was to become used to, in years to come, in second-
rate cowboy and Indian movies. The tinkers had obviously
had a high old night in the pub in Tarbert while the rest of the
community were attending the Saturday evening prayer meeting. And the tinkers could afford a night out; they made money
out of their domestic tin-smithing, they still sold their pots and
pans and milk pails, they lived off the country, they probably
collected dole money by forging signatures on the red-printed
application forms; and, of course, they stole. Now there was a
bloody fight in progress. It appeared to be between two families
because men and women were involved, twisting and weaving
in among the sailcloth tents backlit by the huge peat fires
which had been freely fuelled from the township peat stacks.
I stopped transfixed. The women were the archetypal witches
of my story books as they clawed at their opponents with their
talons or pulled a female enemy to the ground by her hair and
then smashed a bare foot into her belly; the men were using
their fists by and large, but one, older than the rest, was laying
about him with a club of some sort and I could swear that here
and there I saw a knife flashing. The screaming must have
carried to the villages but, of course, nobody would pay any
attention; it was something they were used to on occasional
Saturday nights during the summer. The language was lurid.
I thought I had heard most of the colourful words in the Gaelic
vocabulary by that stage, but it was obvious that my education
had been sadly monitored. I stood transported, soaking up
words and phrases that would dazzle Gillespie when I got
back home at the end of the holiday.

I felt the scalp rising from my head when hands gripped me
out of the dark.

'And where do you think you're going, cove?'

I was pinioned between two wicked-looking youths a head
taller than myself; one of them with two missing teeth where
their absence was most noticeable, and the other with a scar
running from below his greasy long hair to his jawbone.

'H-h-home,' I managed to stutter.

'And since when did you set up home here?' The other thought the joke was uproariously funny.

'I don't mean that.' My mouth was dry and I could hardly get the words out. 'I live with my grandfather in the big house down at the shore. He's a big man,' I added lamely, a statement whose only possible virtue in the circumstances was that it happened to be true.

'Oh, he's a big man is he?' I writhed at my voice being mimicked and the Harris genteelity of it being held up to ridicule by this ruffian. 'Well you tell your Granda that we've got big men here too if he wants to come and visit us. But on second thoughts you better not. In fact you better not even mention that you passed this place tonight because if we hear that you've said a word about what you saw here tonight we'll boot your arse so hard that you'll go sailing over your Granda's big house right out into the middle of the bay. Got it, cove?' And to prove that he meant business he put his foot against my backside and sent me flying. I picked myself up, and not even Tam o'Shanter's mare would have caught up with me as I raced for Big Grandfather's house. I stopped outside the door, waiting for my heart to steady, and I winced when I felt a stabbing pain under my ganzie. And then, relief! It was the tin my cousin had given me; it was still safely there and I must have hurt my rib on it when the tinker boy sent me flying. From inside the house there came the sound of hymn singing. That was a good thing. It meant that Big Grandfather wouldn't be able to say anything to me in front of his worshipping guests; tomorrow was the biggest Sunday of the year, and by Monday his wrath at my late homecoming would have died down.

I slipped into the house and crept upstairs to my own attic bedroom which, as my cousin had guessed, had been commandeered for the duration of the Communion by the two holy old women he had described as 'the two Lewis crones'. I got down on my knees beside the bed and found the handle of the china chamber-pot, the one with the red and yellow roses painted on it. It was empty, as I knew it would be, because Granny was a meticulous housekeeper. But to make sure it was bone dry I gave it a thorough wipe with an old shirt of Grandfather's left there for polishing shoes. I then tipped into the pot the contents of the tin of *Andrew's Effervescent Liver Salts* that my cousin had given me, and went downstairs to join the worshippers, hiding the empty tin in the cubby-hole on my way past. My grandfather looked at me over the gold rims of his spectacles, but there was nothing he could say without interrupting the spiritual voyage of 'The Ark of the Covenant', which was the hymn being sung with shut-eyed fervour by the dozen or so visitors. The Saturday evening domestic prayer meeting was a fringe event of the great Communion festival itself. It was a relaxed affair at which lay hymns were sung instead of the psalms (the equivalents of "The Old Rugged Cross" or "Morning Has Broken", which would not find a place in any formal Gaelic presbyterian service). I would have enjoyed myself fine once upon a time, but my enthusiasm for singing had been diminished since Miss Bassin had put the seal of officialdom on my incompetence in that direction. Saturday night was an unwind; a relax before the great day of Communion Sunday itself, most of which would be devoted to long services and spartan celebration of the Last Supper. The hymn singing finished in time for copious cups of tea to be served before one last prayer was said, so that everybody could be in bed by midnight.

I must have caught the last half hour of the service and it was only the thought of tea that kept me awake after my day on the moor and the excitement of the journey home. I watched the two holy old women of my bedchamber savouring cup after cup of Granny's strong brew, smiling to myself, but as soon as the last prayer was over I slipped off to my cubby-hole lest Big Grandfather be reminded to corner me and challenge me with my lateness.

I lay on my makeshift truckle-bed listening to the men slipping out to the end of the house 'to see what kind of night it was'; Grandfather had not yet installed the bathroom which, a few months later, would take over the cubby-hole in which I now lay. I knew that the women would be lifting their skirts behind the peat-stack at the other end of the house, and I hoped that the two holy women had drunk enough tea to make

84

their bladders trouble them a second time before morning. One by one people came back into the house and, with whispered 'Good nights', they slipped off to their crowded quarters throughout the house. I knew that my grandparents had surrendered the two double box-beds in their own bedroom and would be having yet another cramped night on the couch in the living room. The peace of what was by now the Sabbath morning descended on the house, and only an occasional snore from somewhere disturbed the tranquillity, and the rare miaou of a seabird haunting the moonlit ebb at the foot of the croft.

I was on the point of falling asleep when I heard the bed in the room above my cubby-hole creak, and a mumbling voice as one of the two occupants presumably apologized to her neighbour for disturbing her. I heard a gentle clink as the rose painted chamber-pot was pulled from under the bed, an audible sigh and a moment of silence. And then all hell broke out. The old woman upstairs screamed and called on the Almighty. Her companion shouted at her, startled, enquiring what was wrong. 'The Devil's work!' she yelled. 'A judgment on me!'

'More like a case for the doctor!' shouted her friend.

Then cries for help, and all over the house doors began to open. With my glee stifling me, but keeping my face straight, I went out to the lobby where Big Grandfather was standing with a lit candle in his hand, and from all over the house sleepy-eyed men of God were appearing in their shirt-tails looking like Old Testament prophets hearing the earth shake around Jericho. Modesty was thrown to the winds as everybody crowded upstairs, flannel nightgowns mingling with shirt-tails. Being smaller I managed to squeeze up beside the banister just as the frothy trickle from the attic bedroom reached across the linoleum of the landing and began to trickle downstairs round bare old feet. People crowded into the little bedroom ignoring the modesty of the one standing in the middle of the floor, oblivious to the fact that she still had her nightdress gripped round her knees like a tentative Blackpool wader, and to the one in bed with the bedclothes hugged to her chin. All eyes were on the rose painted peepot which was foaming like a cauldron out of *Macbeth*. Then, as the froth died away, the tumult turned to puzzlement and sympathy, while the victim protested that she had been feeling in perfect health and that such a thing had never happened to her before. Yet one or two looked at her askance as they made their ways back to their disturbed slumbers, and Big Grandfather looked askance at me.

Matters of earthly import weren't discussed on the morning of Communion Sunday no matter how out of the ordinary they might be. People were up early to await their turns for hot water for their ablutions, and to allow each other elbow room for climbing into their Sunday bests. The women helped Grandmother prepare breakfast and, by half past eleven we were all setting off to church in our twos and threes so as to arrive there for eleven o'clock, God's time. The church did not acknowledge British Summer Time which was an unwarranted tampering with God's long-standing subdivisions of the day.

The church was crammed to capacity, as always on Communion Sunday, and heavy with the atmosphere of sanctity spiked with the sharp smell of mothballs. Four ministers, including the local one, were in charge of proceedings, flanked by a cohort of elders which included distinguished men from other parishes. In the Hebrides, and in much of the Highlands still, only a small minority actually participate in the celebration of Communion – men and women who are deemed by their peers worthy to partake of the sacrament, and, more importantly, who deem themselves worthy, something which struck me then and has always struck me since as being paradoxical in view of the humility which is supposed to be one of the keystones of the Christian ethic. The vast majority, attending all the services over the five days with devotion and sincerity, take their places in the wings on Sunday hoping, presumably, that when the Great Day comes the final arbiter will be less selective. The service was, as usual in those days, four hours long as some patriarchs prayed and others testified. I sat, wedged between my grandparents, hearing a sentence here and there, scanning the church furtively for a glimpse of red hair in the vicinity of the doctor's pew, puzzled that my cousin – usually so wise in the ways of the world – should have forgotten that one of the female prerequisites for church attendance was a very large concealing hat!

It was, as always, a long and wearing day. We just had time to walk back home for the very special lunch of Communion Sunday before returning to church again for the evening service. It was a day on which no work whatsoever was done – even less than that permitted on a normal Sunday. In fact I think that the milking of the cow and the feeding of the hens (such as remained of them after the four days of banqueting) were the only two deeds that qualified for exemption under 'the seventh day rule' as *works of necessity and mercy*. Needless to say, modesty – as much as the patent inadmissibility of such a subject for Communion day conversation – precluded any reference to the events of the night before, and by Monday it was forgotten in the rush of preparation for departure after the Monday morning service. Forgotten by all except my grandmother, who took one second to put two and two together when she discovered an empty tin of *Andrew's Effervescent Liver Salts* in the cubby-hole as she strove wearily to restore the house to normality when the last visitor had left. It was probably my imagination that made me think that some of the pious visitors had a stern look in their eyes as they bid me goodbye and wished God's blessing on me in tones which suggested that I needed not only His blessing but His mercy; and it was probably that same overactive imagination which conjured a twinkle in the eyes of those whom one would normally be tempted to believe walked closest to God.

But there was no twinkle in Big Grandfather's eye. 'There was a time,' he said, 'when I used to look forward to your coming here on holiday; but I've spent the last two or three years wondering what the Devil was going to find for you to do next. This house has always enjoyed a reputation as a house of hospitality; its name will now go far and wide as a place where holy old women can't sleep in safety and Heaven knows how that story will get twisted in the telling.' He said a lot more than that, and the business of having had to moderate his language for five days meant that his vocabulary was supercharged. He refrained from packing me off home, but forbade me to leave the confines of the croft for a full week,

'Nor must that skinnymalink of a cousin of yours come near you! If you were my own son instead of my daughter's I would have your trousers down and your backside as red as a boiled lobster!' His own son, one of the heroes of my boyhood, was at that precise moment somewhere off Newport Island, America, aboard *Endeavour II* which was preparing to challenge for the Americas Cup.

Chapter Eight

'RUN down and bring me up a pail of oysters from the shore,' my grandmother would sometimes say. She could read and write English rather laboriously but not, apparently, enough to know whether there was an 'r' in the month. I think she had been to Glasgow once to visit a sister in the Highland enclave of Govan, but she would have confined her explorations to a few well-known landmarks like Wilson's Zoo, the Botanical Gardens and Sauchiehall Street; she wouldn't have been to any posh restaurants and so she wouldn't see anything wrong in boiling oysters till they opened, then rolling them in oatmeal and frying them to eat with potatoes.

Or her eagle eye would spot a huge skate left behind on the Yellow Reef by the tide, stranded by its own weight of eggs in their leathery pouches. 'Quick before the seagulls get at it, and take something to wrap round its tail in case it gives you a nasty hurt!' It was always a race with the seagulls but I never lost because the seagulls had long since learnt that a stranded skate could give a very vicious swipe with its spikey tail. Sometimes it took all my strength to drag the brute all the way up from the shingle shore (the Northlands had no beaches like those of home) but once I got it up to the house it was guarantee of a good meal for several days. Unlike most fish the skate is better left hanging for a day or two. There were all sorts of crude legends about skate because the female ones had some remarkable human resemblances anatomically; fishermen wouldn't eat skate before going off on long fishing trips because they were supposed to be very aphrodisiac. Perhaps the fishermen were right. . . .

The Northlands didn't suffer as much from the Depression as we did, just as the Southlands suffered little in comparison with the cities of the mainland. The Northlands, for one thing, were surrounded by rich seas fit for fishing, while our Atlantic coast was wind-lashed at the best of times and we couldn't very easily manage boats. But apart from that the people of the Northlands had evolved their own survival methods over generations, and they were more self-sufficient than we had yet had time to become. Although they had moved into a money economy just as we had done, they had graduated to it around a market centre with a hotel and offices and shops which generated an essential minimum of jobs, and even the wages of one girl working as a waitress in the hotel or as a clerkess in an office could make a colossal difference to a family with even a tiny patch of land such as they had and exploited to the full in the Northlands; the shops would buy eggs from people like my grandmother to sell to people in the administrative ranks in Tarbert while my mother, in the south, couldn't sell eggs because everybody around had hens of their own. In short the Northlands were reaping the benefits of a minuscule mixed economy with their aged traditional modes of life being underpinned by the money beginning to turn over in an adapting society. There were other factors too, and ways in which the overcrowded conditions which had sent us south were working in favour of the generation that had stayed behind: instead of being able to get land as we had done, many of the other younger ex-servicemen, or those who had been just too young to go to war, were driven to seek work in the cities; and now, with the country's economic upturn beginning to be felt more quickly in the cities than in the islands, those people in the cities or in the merchant navy were able to send cash home to their old parents. We who had appeared to be the fortunate ones were now beginning to feel that fate had dealt us a yarborough.

Big Grandfather was a man of his word, and when he said that I was to be confined to the croft for a week I knew that there would be no remission. But he was also a man of extremely soft heart especially where I, his first-born grandson, was concerned. So, unobtrusively, he went out of his way to make the period of my detention as easy as possible. He involved me in countless pleasant little jobs round the croft, like tarring the roof of a shed, fishing for cuddies off the Yellow Reef when he deemed the tide to be safe, searching the croft morning and night for lambs that might be getting into trouble for one reason or another. It is a fact, common to city and to croft, that work which is a bore and a chore for parents is a pastime when they're being performed for somebody else. And Big Grandfather could be excellent company; he had been in the militia in peacetime, and he had sailed for years as a young crewman on rich men's yachts, so he had fascinating yarns to tell. He had always followed Britain's efforts to recapture the Americas Cup and he knew all about the efforts made by people like Sir Thomas Lipton with his *Shamrocks*; and now here was his own son involved in the most hopeful attempt yet, an attempt to be made by T. M. Sopwith with *Endeavour II*, on which he had spent close on two hundred thousand pounds. Sopwith had strong ties with the Northlands; his yachts *Vita* and *Philante* had been regular visitors to the anchorage below my grandfather's croft, and both of them had been skippered by a Harrisman from next door. So there was plenty to talk about.

On the Monday when my detention order expired I was allowed to take the road over to Wee Grandfather's house where my cousin was waiting to greet me with joy. In no time we were out on the hill, and as we lay in a shady little hollow smoking and rigging our fishing rods I regaled him with all that had happened. He took the success of the chamber-pot episode as a personal triumph for himself, as well he might since he had instigated it and provided the machinery for it, and he began to rack his brains for some means of trying it out himself. It wasn't easy because their house was much smaller than Big Grandfather's and the visitors they had tended to be relatives who used 'the outside' before going to bed. He was a bit disparaging about my failure to dispose of the evidence. 'You're a bitch of a fool,' he said, using one of the best swear phrases in the vernacular.

'You're not all that clever yourself, asking me to look out for a red-headed pusher in church when you might have remembered that every woman in church would be wearing a hat!'

'Hell,' he said. 'I never thought of that. So you didn't see her eh? Well I can tell you something, boy. I've seen her in Tarbert outside the doctor's house, and she's a beauty. A Skye woman. They don't make them like that in Harris. She's about as tall as I am and as slim as a rake except that she's got headlamps like a bus. And she's easy! I'm telling you. Jocky Kerr and Calum Marion have both had a go, and I'm telling you I'm going to find an excuse to get into Tarbert as soon as I find out when she's got her evening off. Just for once I wish school was open. . . . I'm cut off here with no proper excuse to go to the village. . . .' He waxed eloquent for ages, and certainly if even half of what he claimed to have heard was true the doctor's Skye maidservant was 'a bombshell'.

That conversation changed the atmosphere of the whole day. We ate the food that we had brought with us and began fishing till our stomachs told us it was time to go home. I had been given permission to stay and have my tea in Wee Grandfather's and the only condition laid down was that I should be back in Big Grandfather's by eleven o'clock without fail. In view of the diplomatic situation prevailing there I thought the terms quite reasonable and I was determined to be back on schedule.

Big Grandfather, as I have said elsewhere, was married to dumpy little 'Wee Granny', and 'Big Granny' (who was Great Aunt Rachel's sister and built on the same scale) was married to 'Wee Grandfather'. A more disparate set of grandparents one could not find short of carefully arranged marriage contracts between Lilliput and Brobdingnag. But each of the four was an individual personality of considerable consequence. 'Wee Grandfather' (from whom my father took his equanimity I'm sure) was one of the gentlest characters I have ever met, and where Big Grandfather was respected in the community, Wee Grandfather was loved. He was a weaver to trade, and a story-teller of rare quality. He spoke only Gaelic and I've never forgotten the shock I got when I asked him one day – long before the day I'm talking about – to tell me what the caption was to one of the pictures in Arthur Mee's *Children Encyclopaedia*, which my cousin and his sister had got from somewhere and which I coveted beyond all else. 'Ah, my darling,' he said. 'I can't read.' Up till then I had taken it for granted that all adults could read English. But anything he lost through his inability to read he made up for fully with his gift of narrative. And like my father, he was never loth to lay down what he was doing and embark on a story. And so, after the evening meal, the hours flew by and, with a start, I realized that I would have to move pretty smartly if I was to reach my Big Grandfather's by quarter to eleven which, my cousin had slyly suggested, would be a good tactical move on the first day of my new-found freedom.

I set off. The evening light was fading and giving way to a brilliant full moon as I jogged along the road. This was another aspect of the moorlands which flanked the road all the way. Big rocks cast shadows and gave contour to the view; the burns actually tinkled over the shingle; the mountains formed a tall dark ring like the walls of an amphitheatre except for one break in the east through which one could see the Minch like a sheet of undisturbed mercury stretching all the way to the mountains of Skye. In the way that they always do, the mountains seemed to be trapping the moonlight so that I felt as if I were moving through a pool out of which I'd emerge at the other side. Any such poetic thoughts were banished when I realized that I was almost at the tinker encampment and I moved on to the heather verge by the roadside and slowed down so that I made less noise. I shuddered inwardly at the memory of the fellow with the lank greasy hair and the scar running down his cheekbone; if ever there was a candidate for the gallows he was one. But all was quiet. I could see lamp or candlelight coming from each of the tents and, in an occasional one where the flap was open, I could make out a glowing fire with dark figures round it. But the murmur of voices was peaceful, and if I didn't know better from experience I could have made myself believe that I was seeing a colony of the eccentric English tourists who occasionally came to our island to spend summer weeks under canvas in the most outlandish places. But I did know better, and I was glad when the encampment was safely behind me and the voices had disappeared. I resumed my leisurely jogging and, without meeting a living soul, I covered the remaining mile and reached the gate at the top of the path to my grandfather's house. I turned down to the gate and stopped. I couldn't believe my eyes. There, exactly as my cousin had described her, was the willowy red-head with her headlamps, as he had called them, resting on the top bar of the gate as she gazed moodily out across the Minch. I felt the saliva thickening in my mouth. She obviously hadn't heard me, and with my heart thumping in a highly erratic rhythm I muttered 'Excuse me' in English and leant forward to open the gate.

She turned towards me smoothly, without a hint of surprise or hurry and the red of her hair caught the moonlight. She smiled a white provocative smile.

'Excuse me!' she said. 'And since when did Harris boys start speaking English?'

'I didn't know you spoke Gaelic,' I mumbled, feeling myself caught wrong-footed.

'As good as your own,' she said quietly as she stepped aside.

I unhasped the gate and was half-way through it when she spoke again.

'Do you not have much time for girls then, or is it that you like plumper chickens?'

My tongue felt as if it was trapped in syrup, and the tightness in my solar plexus was spreading rapidly to my groin.

'I think you're fine,' I said.

I wished I'd read more of my mother's magazines.

'Are you not going to ask me in then?'

'Ask you in! I live with my grandparents and they'll be going to bed.'

'There are beds and beds,' she whispered coming up so close to me that I could smell a gentle heathery aroma off her hair. 'The bracken's nice and dry on the hillside down there, and there's a place you can't see from the road.'

'I can't be long,' I managed to stutter, 'they'll be waiting for me.' It sounded not only inept but cowardly as well.

'It won't take long,' she said in the same whisper, slipping her arm through mine and, with what I'd taken to be her shyness now completely gone, she led me confidently off the path and down the side of the hill. We didn't speak another word till we reached the bracken hollow that she'd spoken of, and I was glad to arrive because I was beginning to find walking more difficult. When we reached it I stood like an idiot wondering if the laws of etiquette which dictated that one always waited till a lady sat down also decreed that the lady lay down first. She solved the problem for me by flinging herself down and dragging me down after her.

She had lips that scorched and a tongue that darted like an elusive minnow. They were no longer headlamps that rubbed up against me but tantalizing, large, soft breasts that asked to be hurt and yet stopped one short before the point where hurting would have been sin. She was in an ecstasy that I had never known existed, and I was in pain as she rubbed herself closer till I could feel one nipple hard against my chest with the other one like a marble in my hand. She pulled her face away for an instant. Her eyes were closed and her breath was hot on my cheek. 'Downstairs,' she almost spat out. 'Stop wasting time.' I needed no second bidding and all the fantasies of adolescence leapt into a sure experience. My hand slid up and I didn't even notice that she was wearing nothing below her rough tweed skirt; all I felt was a wave of overwhelming giddiness as my fingers found a mound that felt like rough marram grass and the gateway to ecstasy in the middle of it. Her hand had feverishly ripped open the buttons on my trousers and reached inside, when I felt my whole being explode from the waist downwards and a collapse of dignity and everything else. She froze and whipped her hand away as if she had put her hand in a rabbit hole and found a weasel.

'You son-of-a-bitch,' she said. 'You've buggered it!' She wiped her hand on my trousers and jumped to her feet. 'Couldn't you have waited? Or have you never been in before? Or are you one of the ones who's so shit scared there's a bastard at the end of every screw they're happy to spend their lives playing fingers with girls and playing girls with their fingers?'

Not only did she speak Gaelic but she spoke it very fluently and I couldn't even look at her with my face bursting hot with

95

shame and indignity. She was towering above me straightening her clothing, I could sense, and then she came out with the ugliest laugh I'd ever heard; a shrill, harsh laugh that surely couldn't belong to the doctor's maid my cousin had described. It had a shiver of cruelty in it. 'Wait till I tell the boys about the limp-cocked gomeril I found myself tonight!' and she was off over the hill like a hare.

I lay for a few minutes feeling that I was going to vomit, and then I picked myself up and tidied myself as best I could with tufts of bracken and made my way down to the house. My grandfather was on the other side of the door as I opened it.

'Good fellow,' he said. 'You're not so much behind your promised time. I was just going to take a walk up the path to meet you.'

My grandmother was standing at the table with a glass of milk and a plate of oatcakes. She looked at me.

'What's happened to you? Your trousers are wet and your knees are dirty. Did you fall?'

'No,' I said testily. And I felt like adding, 'I tried to but I didn't manage.'

I went to bed fully expecting to lie awake for ages, but I barely managed to pull the bedclothes over my hot face, and, in a few minutes it seemed, Big Grandfather was calling me down to breakfast. The tetchy tone of his voice suggested that it wasn't his first shout.

They had finished breakfast when I got down, and he had obviously 'said the Books'. He always showed a neat economy of time, combining the grace after breakfast with the first prayer of morning worship. He was pulling his second Wellington boot on in order to go milking when a rap came on the door. He craned round to look through the window. 'These damn tinkers,' he said. 'What are they after at this hour of the morning?'

I looked and froze with my porridge spoon half-way to my face. Standing at the door was a big ugly tinker, and with him two people who were presumably his son and daughter; a wicked-looking boy with greasy hair and a scar down the side of his face, and a tall willowy girl with red hair who could never, in the light of day, be mistaken for a maid to the doctor!

'Would you like to buy a new tin for your milking, man of the house?' I heard the familiar silky voice asking my grandfather as he opened the door. Only now it had the well-known tinker whine.

Keeping my back to the window I slid silently and swiftly into the scullery where I stood quaking, remembering stories of the occasional tipsy lad who had wakened up in a ditch, beaten to a pulp because he had made a pass in a drunken moment at a sexy tinker lass. I felt that the big tinker and his son with the scar would not debate any fine issues about who started what. There and then I knew that even if Grandfather did ask me to stay on for the rest of my holiday, the Northlands would not be the place for me to be for the rest of that summer.

Big Grandfather could resist tinker wiles more successfully than I had managed the night before; the tinkers soon left. But I kept close to the croft till Wednesday, and took the bus south on the pretext that I was going to start revising for my bursary which would be coming up next May.

Everybody was very impressed and I got a name for being a swot all of a sudden. My father asked me if it was the Communion which had give me a thirst for knowledge instead of the thirst for righteousness which it was supposed to give. I didn't deign to reply to him, but he was obviously a puzzled man. For my part I kept close to the house except when there was a valid excuse to go up the hill to lift or stack peat, although it was getting near the end of the peat season by then. But even when I appeared most engrossed with my books I always had a weather eye open in case a tinker caravan appeared over the Back of Scarista Hill.

For the only time in my life I was glad when school resumed, and even gladder when the autumn was over and winter came early that year.

Chapter Nine

Big Grandfather had a licence to kill. His contracts were almost all for the Northlands, and for the village of Tarbert in particular, and he was inordinately proud of his steel-barrelled gun, which he kept wrapped in lightly greased flannelette in a mahogany box in a corner of the big oak chest in his bedroom. At least that's where he kept it, safely locked away, when I went north to spend my summer holidays with him; but that was probably because he had never got over the shock of the time that I had banged off the old rusty shot-gun at my grandmother when she was too slow to respond to my demand of 'Hands up!' either because she was sleepy after her Sunday lunch or was unfamiliar with the terminology of Dixon Hawke.

My father had an aversion to guns for a different reason. He had spent four years behind one as a sniper in the First World War and although he would never be drawn in the very slightest on any of his experiences till the day he died, he would never handle a gun or allow one into the house except, very reluctantly, when the days of the Home Guard arrived and all our men were issued with .303 rifles which they kept in their respective attics and produced only for periodic official 'manoeuvres' in the sand dunes or rather less official forays into the deer forest. My father eschewed the latter even more studiously than he attempted to avoid the former because, whatever happened in 'no man's land' those many years ago, he had a deep-rooted and unshakeable aversion to taking life. And when it was necessary to do so he sent for the old man – my grandfather who was, of course, his father-in-law.

That September Big Grandfather didn't come.

I remember it was September because we used to call September 'the month of shoes'. Nothing in our young lives equalled the thrill of the May morning when we discarded our heavy footwear and savoured the first tingle of the unawakened dew except, conversely, the excitement of that brittle September day when our thick stockings and winter boots went on again. By now the May feeling had worn off. Gone was the memory of the first gingerly crossing of the gravel road, the helter-skelter rush across the common grazing land trying to get the blood to course, the flick of the daisies' heads clipping off between soft pink toes, the agonizing pain of a hidden stone going straight from naked sole to heart. By midsummer we could paddle the stoniest bedded stream without a tentative feel for the smoothest surfaces and walk a shingle beach as confidently as shod horses treading turf; and so, through August and the beginning of the hay mow and right up to the return to school, we continued to develop pads that were more like hooves and would be insurance against corns and kindred ailments in the more sophisticated years to come. But come the resumption of classes, with the inevitable curtailment of freedom, and a subtle softening began. And come September, the barefoot freedom began to pall.

The first twinges of frost come early to the Western Isles even though they rarely develop into the deep penetrating hardness of the mainland freeze. Like the sharp little pricklings of myriad needles they come, as the sea begins to get heavy and the heather begins to lose its bloom and the only patches of colour are the cornfields like golden tufts on an ageing counterpane. In those days it was the scythe that laid the corn, and as we got home from school we would cringe inwardly at the sight of the long swathes awaiting us. No time for play. Straight to the cornfield. And the backbreaking monotony of an armful of corn being picked up, its cut ends patted with the palm of the hand to a uniformity, nine or ten stalks whipped out of the parent sheaf and knotted round its middle as tightly as the belt on a blossoming girl. On and on and on it went, with the back getting sorer and stubble underfoot beginning to feel like a carpet of thorns. The autumns had been fun once upon a time, with father keeping up a deliberately inane barrage of banter to spur us on. But father had been becoming very morose of late.

By the time the harvesting had won the race against the frost, and the corn had been stooked and stacked in turn, all 26 young feet in the school were beginning to go through the annual ritual of 'the month of shoes'. The twitches and the wiggles would start during the rhythmic rendering of the Lord's Prayer as the glow generated by the run to school began to wear off. Those of us in the middle class were always the ones to give the first sign; the big fellows wouldn't deign admit to feeling the cold before us and nor would the wee ones dare brave our contempt. But as the days went on the toe-twitching would spread through the whole class-room and extend beyond the '. . . forever, Amen' through the whole long Bible lesson and into the period known as 'Conversation' when we flexed our accumulating knowledge of the English language. Then, as the twitchings developed into the rasping of 26 soles being rubbed stealthily on the wooden floor, the observant onlooker would notice the beginnings of a fraternization of castes at the mid-morning interval, and would realize that 'the month of shoes' was approaching its climacteric. The fraternizing never went beyond the bounds of one theme. Questions would be casually asked and information would be laconically volunteered as to whether Calum the Post had brought a 'C.O.D.', for every boot or shoe worn in our village came from a certain Northampton emporium which had the foresight to distribute foot-charts on which feet were outlined to guarantee accuracy of size when we came to 'walk the Barratt way'.

By the end of September, every home in the village would have received its 'C.O.D.' and on the first Monday in October the school gate would begin to clang earlier than usual. A full quarter of an hour before the whistle blew for line-up a knot of stiff-legged self-conscious males would be assembled in one corner of the playground comparing notes. First to be settled was the question of price. Our parents must have had unlimited resources and the emporium concerned must have made astounding profits because, invariably, the claims put forward would have made even today's city prices seem modest. After price came quality. Here no false bragging could escape challenge. The superiority of boots was judged by the size of the steel plates on toes and heels and the numbers of clusters of three 'tackets' in the soles. The stiffness of the toe-caps was good for a few points, as was the height of the heels and the flexibility of the soles; but armour plating was what mattered most, and that couldn't be put to its final test till night came and it could be adjudged – well away from the ken of parents – who could kick up most sparks from a flat rock or the surface of the road.

That had been the pattern for the few years that I had accumulated, but then came the September when no 'C.O.D.' arrived.

I don't know how the news was broken to me or how I received it. The poverty of the 1930s had crept in on us so subtly that the child, at least, didn't notice it any more than he noticed himself getting taller or his hair grow. The barefoot summer had seemed no different from the rest. The new potatoes had been picked and relished along with the last of the yellowing salt herring from the bottom of the barrel that had seen us through the winter and the spring. Spotty had had a calf which was still with us because it had failed to find a market, and she and Rosie had kept us in a plentiful supply of milk and butter. Once or twice I had noticed that my mother had sent me to the new grocery van which had started doing a weekly round with a pencilled note instead of the usual pound note or the handful of silver, and the driver had grunted and put the note on a nail on top of a pile of others and handed me a single loaf (a 'half loaf' as he called it, instead of a 'quarter', which was – paradoxically – two loaves stuck together), a quarter pound of tea and two pounds of sugar. A boy wasn't to know that that was the maximum to which 'tick' could now be extended, or that mother couldn't summon up the courage to face the grocer herself despite the fact that (or maybe because) they had been schoolmates in their youth. Poverty is different from being broke; poverty doesn't permit of a hope for the future, just as – in retrospect it rarely produces songs, except from those who have only read about it in the history books or have had it interpreted for them in the cause of a political ideology. The person suffering from poverty has merely fallen from a standard of living to which the generations before him have aspired.

In the middle thirties, we in the Hebrides were fortunate – although we didn't see it then – that we hadn't been caught up in the rampaging progress which had been accelerating through the western world since the middle of the nineteenth century, and 'white loaf civilization' was still new enough to us for us to be able to reach back to a way of living which still survived in the older memories. A bowl of oatmeal brose with fresh milk was ample breakfast for a working man; mussels from the sea rocks, boiled till they opened and then rolled in oatmeal and fried would probably be extolled by today's dieticians; dulse seaweed eaten raw might not keep a man alive forever but it probably contained nutrients such as sophisticated health shops now build fortunes on; carrageen seaweed boiled in milk occasionally features in expensive leather-bound menus. All these things were dredged out of the folk memory, but I can understand why people like my parents, who had set out with high hopes to create a new and prosperous life in a new community, felt that the clock was going back for them and that the dawn of their dreamt future was slipping back into dark.

It was Gillespie's mother who had introduced us to sand-eels. The generations of my people who had sojourned in the Northlands before returning to the Atlantic shore and the white beaches had forgotten those long silvery denizens of the wet sand of the ebb. 'When you see the seagulls walking on the sand at the wave mouth, that's the surest sign of a shoal,' she said, and thrusting a rusty serrated sickle into my mother's hand she led us down to the sandy bar left exposed by the low tide. Flexing herself into a crouched position like a hovering wicket keeper, she plunged her sickle into the sand in front of her and drew it steadily towards her with her left hand cupped ahead of it. Nothing happened for the first pull or two but she kept advancing slowly, always slicing into the virgin sand on which we hadn't stepped. And then, suddenly, she jerked the sickle and clenched her left hand round a fistful of wet sand which contained a nine-inch-long eel of shimmering silver and as thick as her thumb. 'There you are,' she laughed triumphantly. 'I told you they were here; they're always here when the seagulls walk on the sand!' Patiently she instructed mother and Gillespie and myself in the art of sand-eel catching, but it was long ago and if I were to claim that I caught one on that first day I'd probably be succumbing to the fisherman's best known failing. But she filled a pail; enough for a good meal for each family. Once she drew her hand away and didn't seize the fish, leaving it to flounder on the surface of the sand instead of flashing back down into it in a blink as the sand-eel did. 'You've got to watch that fellow,' she said, pointing to a thick stubby fish with three vicious-looking spikes in his back. 'That's a *stangarram*; his sting can swell your arm to the shoulder, and he's even been known to kill. But it's not often you come across one, and you'll get to know the heavy feel of him on the sickle.' Sand-eels rolled in flour and fried, linger on the memory's tastebuds as few other things do; I think I'd prefer not to taste one now in case the memory is playing tricks again, but Gillespie and I became reasonably expert at catching them, and pailfulls of them went a long way towards helping us over the lean years. But sand-eels disappear in autumn to wherever sand-eels go.

I accepted that 'the month of shoes' was not going to bring me a pair of new boots that year, and that the sandshoes from spring were going to have to be revived for a month or two. I accepted with bad grace, dreading the humiliation of being different. But there was no 'month of shoes' for any of us. One or two of the boys whose fathers were employed by the Estate may have had new boots but, if so, they must have been well rehearsed not to boast about them. The fire in the school was lit earlier than the statutory 10 October, and if the weather was bad we were encouraged to spend our playtimes grouped round it. It's a peculiarly inconsequential detail to remember – the business of spending playtimes round a schoolroom fire – but there's a reason for the memory which was important of its time. One of the sacrifices some families had to make was the regular copy of the *Daily Express*, but one boy's father had been able to keep his daily paper coming and Farquhar brought the cuttings of Rupert Bear to school each morning, and it was easier to pass them from hand to hand round the fire than in a windy corner of the playground!

The pegs that anchor memories can be as flimsy as the well-thumbed cuttings of the adventures of Rupert Bear, or the noise that made me sit up and take notice from where I sat crouched in the dusk on the corner of St Clement's bench – the long wooden settle which had come from the ancient church at Rodel when it was being refurbished. Tea, as we called the evening meal, was late. Father had gone for paraffin and the lamp couldn't be lit till he returned. Mother was bent over a frying pan, obviously in a bad mood because she had barely spoken since I'd come in from school. I sat sulkily, unable to go out to play because it was too cold; unable to read because it was too dark. And then I became aware of a steady 'phut' and hiss noise which had a regular monotony to it, but which I couldn't identify. Instinctively I looked at the window to see if it was rain on the corrugated iron – which I would have known it wasn't if I'd stopped to think. In any case the noise was coming from the direction of the stove, and when I peered closely I froze. Mother was listlessly turning over some kind of small oatmeal bannocks in the frying pan, staring silently in front of her, and every now and again a tear rolled down her cheek and sizzled on the hot surface of the stove. I couldn't say anything; I didn't have the words or the way. But suddenly all sorts of fragments of hitherto meaningless overheard conversations fell into place for me; I knew that she was crying because she had nothing in the house to cook except those handfuls of oatmeal, and instead of hunger I was overcome by an ungovernable embarrassment and wished to God that my father would come home.

'Well, we'll have light at least,' he said as he came in and took the lamp out to the porch for filling. 'I don't know what I feed a big boy for when I've got to go traipsing a mile to the shop for paraffin.' He sounded cheery, whistling quietly to himself as he filled the lamp, and I knew why; he had met one or two of the villagers and had some conversation with them. Just that. Several times recently I'd heard him complaining of lack of company, and the fact that we rarely had visitors those days. Nobody had. People cease to be sociable when there's little to be sociable about and no hospitality to offer except the kind that would be most welcome.

'That's a bit better!' My mother had whipped the corner of her apron away from her eyes when she saw the light coming into the room, but he noticed and his stride checked momentarily before he continued his walk to the table with the lamp. He turned the two wicks up slowly so as not to crack the glass funnel, and as he turned round his hand went automatically to his pocket for his pipe which I knew would be empty unless somebody had given him a 'cut' of tobacco while he was out. He stood looking at my mother for a few moments and the strained little smile couldn't make its way to his eyes.

'So that's it, is it? It's come to this. Well, that settles it. I'm going to kill Betsy tonight. I was going to send for the old man tomorrow, but I'm not going to watch you going through this any longer. I don't like doing it, but that's that!'

Betsy! I was too stunned to speak, and past the age of crying. Betsy was the pet sheep I had helped to bottle feed the year I'd first gone to school; she had lost her own mother, and, having been brought up on the bottle she had never taken to going to the moor or the machair grazing with the other sheep, choosing instead to hang around the croft and steal hay from the stackyard in winter. Her last two lambs had been stillborn, and with the tweed market in the doldrums even her fleece wasn't of any practical use. Deep down I had known for long enough that her days were numbered, but I had always assumed that father would try to sell her, or, at the very worst, that Big Grandfather would arrive with the mahogany box containing his gun, the humane killer which some new-fangled law had made it compulsory for him to have in his capacity as part-time butcher to the Tarbert shop. But here was father going to do the job himself, although I knew he hated it. And I knew who would be called on to stir for him.

'Poor Betsy,' my mother said, looking relieved nevertheless. 'I'll be sorry to see her go. But there's nothing for it; there isn't another scrap in the house. You'll manage?'

I wondered at the concern in her voice; at that time I hadn't realized the depth of my father's aversion to killing.

'Of course!' he said gruffly. 'The big fellow here will give me a hand,' he added, looking at me. 'But we'll leave it till the young one's in bed.' I didn't know where my brother was – he was probably in the bedroom playing with the baby – but I was secretly glad for him that he wasn't around. By morning, when the deed would be over, he would view the carcase quite dispassionately and probably ask if he could have the horns to play with, or forget it as quickly as I had forgotten the killing of the hens for Mary's wedding feast. Such was the pragmatism of the country boy of those days. And may be still.

My brother created the usual fuss about being sent to bed before me, but at last he was tucked in and – despite inevitable protests about not being sleepy – he was dead to the world in minutes. Patently trying to conceal his reluctance, my father lit the storm lantern and prepared to go to the byre. 'Give me a few minutes and you follow on with the pail and the spirtle,' he muttered to me as he went out. My mother emptied one of the white enamel pails that was normally used for drinking water, dried it, put a handful of salt in the bottom of it, and handed it to me along with long-handled wooden stirring spoon. By the time I reached the byre father had Betsy trussed on a wooden trestle with her head hanging over the end of it to expose her neck, and he was giving his pocket knife a final rub on the whet stone.

I had often helped Big Grandfather slaughtering sheep for the Tarbert shop, but that was a much more impersonal affair. His gun was styled exactly like a pistol except that there was a gap between the barrel and the loading breech so that it couldn't be fired till the end of the barrel was placed against the back of the victim's head, between the horns, and pressed till the gap closed; the instant the gap was closed the trigger was pressed and the animal was dead before it was bled. But this was different. Betsy winced slightly as father slashed the jugular vein but, thereafter, she seemed to feel no pain as she lay watching me as I stirred the blood flowing into the enamel pail to get the salt through it and keep the blood from congealing so that it could be used for black puddings; it was only as the pail neared its fill and the pulsing flow slowed to its final trickle that she must, for one split second, have felt life leaving her; she gave one frightened little grunt and it was all over. The rest was routine – the skinning and the gutting; the separation of the liver which would be tomorrow's meal; the final cutting off of the head, which would be hung for a couple of days before being singed and made into sheep's head broth. Not one scrap would be wasted. Next day mother would empty and scrub the stomachs and the intestines in the river and stuff them for a variety of puddings – black, oatmeal, and flour and currant. Even the skin, with the wool still short from the summer shearing, would be cured and dried to serve as a bedroom rug for a while.

Betsy, jointed and salted in a pickle strong enough to float an egg would have seen us through a bit of the winter, but it was when we were hauling up the carcase by its hind legs to hang it from the byre rafter that I noticed a pile of rusting gin traps lying in a corner. My father and I hadn't exchanged a word till then.

'Why don't we trap rabbits?' I asked. 'Other people do.'

'Ach, I don't know. I was thinking about it; that's why I got the traps. But I'm not much of a hand at it; I wasn't used to it.'

Sure enough there weren't many rabbits in the Northlands from which we'd come, and the ones that were there were wiry little things that lived in scraggy burrows in among the rocks where it was difficult to get at them. But the rich machair lands of the new village were alive with rabbits – big strong fat ones, living off the lush meadowland and the crofters' crops. The landlord, at some point, had imported a large batch of black Dutch rabbits to strengthen the breed, and – although the black strain could now only be detected in a darker than usual tinge of the fur – the machair rabbits were as big as hares and one of them was a full meal for a family of five. We weren't supposed to kill them even when they pillaged the corn or the cabbage patch because they were classed as 'game', but our cat, Tiger, wasn't well versed in the laws of crofting tenure and in the spring and summer we were likely to find as many as half a dozen unblemished dead rabbits lying neatly laid out on the doorstep some mornings. Tiger was a great hunter but a fastidious eater and he preferred to have his catch gralloched for him, provided he was rewarded for his labours with what he considered the delicacies – the livers and the hearts! So although they were technically forbidden to us, we were no strangers to rabbit stew during the good weather when the bucks and the bigger young ones were good eating, although the does were out of season. There are few more delicious dishes than jointed rabbit rolled in flour, fried in butter to a deep brown and then simmered with onion and carrot. And rabbit soup thickened with cornflour and seasoned with water-cress and dulse is gourmet fare. But, unfortunately, Tiger was a fine weather hunter, and in the winter his expeditions were confined to the stackyard where his catches were more to his taste than ours. Poor Tiger! There was no way of salving his wounded feelings by explaining that there was a subtle difference, in the realms of human gastronomy, between a plump rabbit and a fat rat.

'Can I go trapping?' I asked my father.

'You'd take the fingers off yourself.' He was only half listening as he mopped up the strains of blood and the wisps of wool.

'No, I wouldn't. I know how to do it. Look!' And I sprang a gin trap with my heel, latched the right hand jaw, fine set it, and lowered the left jaw.

'Look at that. A fly couldn't walk over that!'

'You're right at that.' He looked at me quizzically. 'So that's how the gin traps were always lying scattered about. You've been practising, eh? Well you better not tell your mother till you've brought your first rabbits home, or she'll be imagining you without an arm, far less a hand! And don't get caught or you'll get me evicted for poaching!'

'How can *you* be evicted if *I'm* the one doing the poaching?'

'Oh, stop arguing for God's sake and take that pail of blood into the house!'

Of course he wouldn't be evicted for poaching a rabbit, but it was better not to cross the landlord unnecessarily. I wasn't to know that it was the killing of the sheep that had put my father's nerves on edge.

'Father's in a bad mood again!' I said to my mother as I handed her the pail.

'Ach, poor man, he hasn't had a smoke for two days. But the dole will be here tomorrow and you can over to the shop and buy him an ounce. Many a man would complain more than he does. Wash your hands and get to bed now; you'll be even more like a ghost than usual in the morning.'

She filled a basin from the brass tap on the Modern Mistress stove and I scrubbed my hands with white Sunlight soap till they were red and raw, but they were still smelling of blood and tallow as I climbed in beside my brother.

'We're going trapping tomorrow!' I said in a loud whisper, but he was away in the depths beyond dreams. I lay awake for a long time planning which warrens to start with, and scheming how to outwit the rabbits when they would start coming out of their burrows at dusk and at dawn. Life was good again; there would be a good feed tomorrow and there was adventure on the horizon. The memory of Betsy's last gurgle makes me squeamish now, but I fell asleep that night without giving my erstwhile pet lamb a second thought.

Chapter Ten

I T would be foolish to pretend to remember that I spent that autumn night dreaming of the assault that was about to begin on the rabbit population of the sand dunes, and daft to pretend to know whether or not they huddled in their families, deep in their sandy burrows, shivering from premonitions of impending doom. What I do know is that they gained an unexpected reprieve. I was wakened at cold first light by a great hubbub. The baby was ill and in danger of dying, according to my mother. The baby was sick but in no danger of dying, according to my father – who was, nevertheless, in an unusual state of panic padding backwards and forwards between the living room and the bedroom with basins of water and towels. The 'baby' was a muscular two-year-old by then, but he still slept with my mother and father in the big double bed which was at right angles to the equally big double bed shared by my other brother and myself. I had resented the belated arrival ferociously, and doubly resented the fact that, during the summer months and the sunny days of play, I was forever being lumbered with him when I would rather have been roaming the beach or the lower reaches of the moor with Gillespie.

From somewhere or other a contraption called a go-chair had appeared – probably a secondhand gift from some cousin of my mother's who had abandoned child-bearing – and if the day was bland at all (indeed if it was the kind of day that Gillespie and I would class as ideal for a ploy) then, as sure as the turning of the tide, I would be detailed to take the baby with me and 'be sure not to wander far out of sight of the house'. It was enough to lose any twelve-year-old his dignity, and it would certainly have been enough to lose me my best friend if he had been someone of lesser loyalty. But Gillespie was not only loyal but resourceful as well. He it was who discovered that with the baby out of it the go-chair would fold flat like a toboggan on four wheels, and that, lying flat, face downwards on it, we could career down the machair slopes at breath-taking speeds while the baby gurgled happily on the green sward chewing on daisies or buttercups or whatever else took his fancy. 'We better keep the little bugger clear of rabbit droppings,' said Gillespie, 'or your mother will knock the devil out of us if he goes home with his mouth black with shit.' We were beginning to pride ourselves on a fluent adult vocabulary which we were careful to exercise only privately between ourselves. We had worked hard to win my mother's confidence, and she had ceased to worry when we began to disappear with our charge over the lip of the big hollow down on the seaward edge of the machair. She was less inclined to agitate when she knew that we were within hearing distance if she shouted; she would have been less joco had she seen her newest infant being dumped the moment we were out of sight, and his carriage being converted into our version of *Bluebird* – which had rocketed Sir Malcolm Campbell to fame on Salt Lake Flats, Utah, a year or two before. I think it was fun with the go-chair which had first and finally broken down my childish jealousy of the baby, and now, watching him retch his little heart out, I felt sorry for him and more than a little afraid.

The drama must have been in progress for some time before I wakened and slithered out of bed in my shirt-tails to watch the puking infant who was, by now, beginning to slump with sheer exhaustion in my mother's arms. She was wiping away the froth that kept forming on his lips while my father mopped away half-heartedly at the remains of the sickness on the bedclothes, leaving behind an unmistakable red tinge.

'He's lost an awful lot of blood,' said my mother hoarsely. 'Go for the doctor right away; I'm scared another bout will be the end of him. O God what's brought this on us?'

Deep down in the islander's conscience there still remained in those days, and to a certain extent even now, the lingering superstition that physical ailment is some form of Divine retribution.

'Don't let me hear you talk like that, woman.' My father's gruffness was a pretence at confidence which even I could sense wasn't very surely founded, and an effort to bolster up her morale. 'It'll turn out to be something he's eaten, and tomorrow we'll be laughing at ourselves. But I'll go for the doctor just to put your mind at ease; and just to make sure he comes I'll go for him myself. You,' he said, turning to me in a sudden burst of decision, 'get your trousers on and go and borrow James's bicycle for me and then get yourself and your brother ready for school!'

The doctor! He obviously thought the matter was serious when it was the doctor he was thinking of summoning and not the nurse. And James's bicycle! I didn't know that my father could ride a bicycle. But I yanked my trousers and jersey on, remembering in the nick of time to slip my old sandshoes on as well, and I set off running down the road.

'The baby's dying,' I yelled to Farquhar the roadman who was trudging along with his pick and shovel on his shoulder and a cloud of his aromatic pipe tobacco trailing along behind him on the brittle autumn air. 'Father wants James's bicycle to go for the doctor.' I was aware of him stopping and trying to find words to say, but words didn't come quickly to him and I sped on.

'The baby's dying,' I gasped to my cousin Mary when she came to the door with sleep still gumming her eyes. 'Father wants James's bicycle to go for the doctor!'

'God save us,' she said. 'It's out in the shed. Be quick with you. I'll be along in a minute to see your poor mother.'

My highly developed sense of the dramatic combined with a new sense of my own importance, blending into a feeling of exhilaration which completely submerged the gravity of the situation; but nothing could dim the sheer ecstasy of having James's coveted bicycle all to myself with his own, or at least his wife's permission. Had James been at home he would rushed it to my father in his underpants rather than let me lay a finger on it; on half a dozen occasions he had threatened to cut my ears off if he ever saw me as much as touching it, after

I had bent his mudguards trying to master the act of riding it while he had been visiting our house. Latterly he had taken to chaining it to the gatepost whenever he called; but James was now in the Persian Gulf, wherever that might be, and the gleaming Raleigh and I were legitimately alone. It seemed only sensible to try to get some practice in. My experiments were not entirely successful and I have no idea which was more scraped, the bike or I, by the time I became aware of my father striding towards me flushed with anger. 'I might have known it!' he thundered. 'Just wait till I get back home, and then wait again till James comes back from sea!' He snatched the bicycle from me and whipped it round. I stared open mouthed as he put his left foot on the pedal, kicked twice with his right, swung himself effortlessly into the saddle and with the slightest of preliminary wobbles set off scorching down the road, sending the gravel flying in his wake. Old men had hidden talents, I mused to myself as I made my crestfallen way home.

My brother was finishing his breakfast as I got in. Mother was up and dressed and much more composed, although I could see that she was still worried as she mixed my bowl of brose, sprinkled some sugar on it and drowned it in milk. 'What in the name of Goodness have you been telling people?' she asked. 'Farquhar the roadman's been here wanting to go for a minister. Before I know where I am the neighbours will be crowding here as if for a wake. I wish you would learn to stop making a saga out of an incident! Get your brose inside you and get to school!' She picked up a plate of something and went through to the bedroom while I sat down by my brose trying to ignore the smug grin that my brother always reserved for my moments of greatest discomfiture.

We had missed 'the line' by the time we got to school but, uncharacteristically, the schoolteacher made no comment as we slid into our seats, and she asked for no explanations. 'Stand up,' she said. 'And close your eyes.' And we launched into the Lord's Prayer as usual, and rattled through it with the incoherence which the Lord, in his infinite mercy, must long since have decided to ignore. 'Take out your Bibles!' It was obvious that nothing was going to be allowed to interfere with the normal routine of the classroom, and I began to feel that my place in the limelight was going to elude me. Had nobody heard? Did crisis and even impending death not matter any more?

The Bible lesson stretched out to its inexorable half hour, but when it was over 'Conversation', appeared for a moment as if it was going to retrieve the situation. 'Farquhar the roadman says that Mrs Macdonald's baby is going to die!' chirruped one of the girls from the Higher Infants, jumping her place in the queue in her excitement to be first with the news, and probably grateful for a Heaven-sent piece of information that would conceal the fact that she had forgotten to prepare a sentence the night before. For a while there had been a rule that sentences produced for 'Conversation' had to begin with the words 'I read in the newspaper . . .' but the rule had been relaxed since money had begun to get scarce and most families had had to forgo the daily paper habit which had just begun to get a hold. There was a gratifying buzz of interest.

'That's enough of that,' snapped Miss Martin. 'Who said it was your turn, Shona? I don't want to hear any more of that kind of talk. We all know that the doctor is going to see the baby and the baby is going to be perfectly all right. Now I want to hear the sentences that you've all prepared!' The dreary routine of fabricated news items went on, with those who had forgotten to do their homework resorting to the usual ruses – trying to get away with mundane comments on the weather of the day or of the week, or trying to slip in a sentence that had been used by somebody days before in the hope that the teacher had forgotten. 'Right,' she said when it was all over. 'It's perfectly obvious I'm going to have to start giving out subjects; some of these sentences are perfectly dreadful. But we'll leave that for the moment and move on. Everybody! What's our morning word?' I felt my face getting hot as the school chorused it.

'Spell it, Finlay!' At least I could do that.

'H-y-g-e-n-e.'

'Wrong! You should be ashamed of yourself. Maggie Jean?'

'H-y-g-i-e-n-e,' simpered a girl two years my junior, and I didn't need the teacher to confirm that she was right.

Hygiene was a concept which had become epidemic in our school in the last few weeks. It had started the year before when a financially crippled Local Authority, forced by national stringency to make us make do with secondhand schoolbooks, had suddenly conjured up enough money to install chemical lavatories which nobody would use, and a row of white wash basins which nobody wanted but which Wm B. Morrison of Glasgow had been eager to supply. In their wake, in the new term, as if alerted to the fact that Scarista School now had brass taps gushing water, a firm called D. & W. Gibbs Ltd had decided to mark the occasion by launching a campaign to save the nation's teeth. And our school was in the firing line.

It was a brilliantly orchestrated operation. It started, if I remember rightly, with the enrolment of all of us as *Crusaders* (with enamel badges to prove our membership) dedicated to the task of defending our *Ivory Castles* against *Giant Decay*! (I hope whoever dreamt up the idea lived to reap an ample share in the profits which have subsequently accrued to D. & W. Gibbs Ltd, even if he did cause me a certain amount of confusion when I came to read of the Christian campaigns in the Holy Land in the eleventh to fourteenth centuries). We had our own monthly newspaper called the *Crusaders' Own Paper*, in those days when our parents couldn't afford the *Daily Express*. It carried horrific stories about the ravages of decay on teeth, disguised of course as the assaults of the fearsome giant on ivory castles throughout the land; it carried articles by *Crusaders* in schools from Lerwick to Land's End, so that we were comforted to know that yellowing teeth were not a prerogative of the Outer Hebrides and that even little Fauntleroys in the Home Counties had gummy grannies too; it carried crosswords and competitions, all of which, subtly, had to do with teeth; but not the least of its journalistic brilliance was that it carried an elegant sufficiency of general news which could be deemed to widen our knowledge and even tempt our more literate parents to browse through it. But nothing was for nothing even then! In order to be a *Crusader* one had to invest in a toothbrush, and in a little round aluminum tin for which D. &. W. Gibbs Ltd were prepared to provide endless supplies of rather pleasant-tasting medallions of pink dentrifrice which we were under oath to use morning, noon, and night after meals. Along with each kit went monthly calendar cards marked 'a.m.', 'mid-day' and 'p.m.' for each day. Parents were put on their honour to tick off the appropriate spaces as proof of evening and weekend brushings, but the responsibility for the morning and mid-day performances was shouldered by schoolteachers up and down the country. And so when Miss Martin said 'Hygiene' and wee Maggie Jean spelt it, that was the signal for us to line up at the brass taps and brush our teeth so that the teacher, on Presbyterian soul and conscience, could put a hygienic little cross on our cards. Although she was prepared to call it a cross, since that was how the *Crusaders' Own Paper* referred to it, she was always careful to draw the symbol of confirmation as a definite *x* so as to absolve herself from any possible hint of fealty to Rome. It was no small tribute to the propaganda skills of the toothpaste company that they were able to involve the educational network of the United Kingdom in their campaign – that teachers could be enticed into supervising it, and, above all, that ragamuffin Hebridean schoolchildren could be cajoled into carting around toothbrushes and tins of dentifrice along with the literary paraphernalia of school. 'Please miss, I have forgotten my toothbrush' was as grievous an admission as 'Please miss, I've forgotten to do my homework.' Forgotten dentifrice wasn't such a desperate affair; a 'rub' could be scrounged from a friend.

But that morning, in the turmoil of the domestic crisis, my brother and I had not only forgotten our toothbrushes and our tins of dentifrice but we had forgotten our registration cards as well, with the result that we had no means of proving that we had fortified our *Ivory Castles* against *Giant Decay* the night before. If truth be told, the fact that we didn't have our cards was reasonable proof that one or other of our parents had certified our fulfilment of our *Crusaders'* oath on the previous evening; otherwise, the cards would have been in among our schoolbooks to be certified by ourselves swiftly and secretly under the lids of our desks or in the privacy of one of the new toilets. Naturally one could hardly lead that as evidence.

This may seem a matter of remarkably small significance to have imprinted itself in such detail on the mind of a man from a lineage of non-toothbrushers which had thitherto reached back to Eden. But it happened to be a very important morning. Each month the *Crusaders' Own Paper* ran an essay competition, divided into sections for defined age groups, on subjects chosen to suit those various groupings; for those qualifying as infants the subject might be as simple as "The pet I would like best" and, for all I remember, there may have been a top grade contest for white-toothed geniuses on "Einstein's Theory of Relativity and its applications to dental hygiene"; what was of particular interest to me was that the prize offered to my age group was, from time to time, a bicycle – the thing which I coveted more than anything else in the whole wide world. Hitherto the subjects had been ones of urban significance in which a school, such as ours, with its total complement of 13, was singularly disadvantaged. But here, at last, was a subject with which everybody could have an equal chance. I can't recall the exact title, and neither, unfortunately, can Messrs Gibbs because their files were destroyed during the Blitz, but it was something like "The Place Where I Live". It was right up my street, if one may be allowed a highly inappropriate phrase, because I had loved and savoured our new village from the moment I had caught my first glimpse of it those seemingly many years ago. I had had a month's notice of the subject because it had been announced in the issue before last, and I had devoted a lot of thought to it. Now here, at last, was the designated morning of the competition, and here was I without the one essential qualification – a fully completed dental card attesting that I had brushed my teeth up and down, and backwards and forwards, morning, noon and night for a whole month. The teacher knew that essay writing was one of my better skills; she knew that I had at least a sporting chance of being in the prize list and a place in the prize list would have been an honour for the school; she knew that I had set my heart on winning. But she had to sign a declaration at the foot of the entry paper that she had, in her possession, the fully completed monthly dental chart of each competing *Crusader* to testify that the contestant had honoured the *Crusaders'* code. She was also on her honour to organize the competition under school examination conditions, starting it punctually at eleven o'clock and uplifting the essays, completed or otherwise, at twelve. And here was her prize contestant without his certificate, with only five minutes to go!

When I saw the teacher glancing at her watch I knew immediately what was going through her mind; she was debating whether, in view of the uncertain circumstances at home, she could give me permission to sprint back to the house, collect my own and my brother's cards, and come back to start my 'piece' – as my journalist friends would now call it – five or ten minutes late. I was on the point of encouraging her towards that decision when she heard the rattle of an approaching car and she looked out of the window. In those days, and particularly on our roads, cars did rattle and they were few and far enough between to cause a minor stampede to doors and windows in most homes. Not in school, of course. Only the teacher could keep track of the passing traffic from her vantage point at her desk.

'Too late, Finlay,' she said. 'I was going to suggest that you could run home and bring your cards, but that was the doctor's car and it wouldn't be right to disturb the family just now.' She paused and communed with her conscience. 'I'll tell you what we'll do though,' she said after one final decisive look at her wrist. 'You'll all get on with your compositions as if everything was normal and then, at dinner time, you, Finlay, will run home for the cards and I'll send a note along with the entries explaining the circumstances and that will keep things in order.' With that she began to hand out the foolscap entry forms so that the last one was dispensed on the stroke of eleven o'clock. It didn't cross my mind to wonder at the complicated brouhaha or to doubt for a moment whether the exalted editor of the *Crusaders' Own Paper* would really sit at his desk in London scanning thousands of hopeful essay entries from all corners of the kingdom and deciding for himself that F. Macdonald of Scaristavore did not ring as true a *Crusader* as his female contemporary M. Roberts of Grantham. What did flash across my mind with a tingle of excitement was that the teacher must have a fair amount of confidence in me to cause her to go to such extremes of effort to align her conscience with the rules; because, after all, not all the entries from every school in Britain were going to cascade into the headquarters of Gibbs – each teacher had to select what was, in her opinion (all teachers were female as far as I was aware then) the best entry in each class and submit it to represent the school. The glory would be the school's but, I suddenly felt sure, the prize bicycle would be mine. And all the tribulations of the morning went out of my mind as I began to write.

The school, like many schools in the Western Isles, had a large oaken bookcase with a brass plaque on it announcing that the library which it contained had been presented, for some reason which I have never been able to discover, by Messrs J. & P. Coats, a famous firm of thread manufacturers in the town of Paisley. It may have been that Messrs Coats had, early on, cottoned on to the benefits of 'diversification' and had decided to invest in some convoluted way in the book trade, and were going to pains to ensure a literate clientèle for the future; or their reasons may have been as obscure and subtle as those which nowadays prompt giant scaffolding companies to branch out into the marketing of books. But, whatever the reason, there is no doubt that that particular area of the beneficence of Coats helped me on my weary journey towards literacy in English and gave me the love of books which has been with me all my life. During our occasional Leisure Periods (euphemistic disguises for occasions when the teacher had private business of her own to transact) we were encouraged to browse through the library, and, under the impression that it was a book of pictures I had seized on one called *Sketch Book* by Washington Irving. It dealt with the adventures of one Rip Van Winkle, personified for me, by old Hector MacGeachan. Washington Irving's lovable hero had also lived in the shadow of the mountains and if I hadn't known that the Catskill Mountains were in another continent I would have sworn from their description that they were the hills of home. It was all there – the blue haze and the mystery which our own mountains represented for me – and the description was so masterly that it seemed wasteful of time and effort for me to try to improve on it, particularly as I was fairly certain that the teacher had never read *Sketch Book* and my instinct told me that the editorial staff of D. & W. Gibbs had not done so either.

And so I laboured lovingly for an hour, adding an original touch and a Gaelic place name here and there and by the time I had finished, having filled both sides of the foolscap page, the essay destined for the desk of the editor of the *Crusaders' Own Paper* was a masterly description of "The Place Where I Live" in my handwriting but in the style and language of Washington Irving – who had almost certainly never brushed his teeth in his life.

The schoolmistress declared a two hour dinner period in reward for our efforts but, probably, also because she wanted to hear news of the baby's welfare and the doctor's diagnosis. I was bidden to run all the way home and come straight back again with my dental record card, my dentifrice, and my toothbrush so that the formalities could be honourably concluded.

As soon as I entered the house I knew that all was well. The baby was sitting on his hunkers in the middle of the floor chewing at a hard crust of bread from the jar in which my mother always stored stuff that would help him with his teething; my father was sitting at the end of the table smoking his pipe and reading a copy of the *Daily Express*, so he had obviously intercepted Calum the Post with the dole Money Order and cashed it; my mother, looking considerably more cheerful than I had seen her for some days, was rolling sliced liver in flour in preparation for frying it for dinner. My brother struck the only discordant note in the otherwise harmonious scene; he was sitting hunched and grim faced on the corner of St Clement's Bench, having raced home while I was being given my final instructions by the teacher.

'How's the baby?' I asked.

'My father didn't look up from his paper. 'The baby's all right, little thanks to you two!'

'Little thanks to us?' I said in genuine perplexity, noticing, nevertheless, that my mother was being singularly uncommunicative as she stood at the table with her back to me. I looked at my brother but he just stared glumly ahead.

'What have we done wrong?'

My father came out from behind his paper and removed his pipe.

'You and your damn tooth scrubbing! That's what's wrong. Your Great Aunt Rachel wouldn't know a toothbrush from a hairbrush and she's as fit as a fiddle at sixty-nine. . . .'

'But Great Aunt Rachel has false teeth that she puts in on Sundays.' I could never resist contradicting him even when I knew it unfailingly made matters worse.

'Shut up! And how often have I told you not to leave things where the wee one can reach them, even though I think he's sometimes got as much sense as the two of you put together. The baby ate two whole damn cakes of that pink dentifrice of yours – that's what the matter was. It's no thanks to you that he's all right, but I've been made to look a fool in front of the whole of South Harris – bicycling off for the doctor at the crack of dawn while Farquhar the roadman's been going round the place telling people the baby's got a plague of some sort! I'm going to be a laughing-stock for weeks, I can tell you; this is one case the doctor won't be afraid to discuss with his cronies!'

'If he's eaten the dentifrice how can I brush my teeth for the competition?'

'I don't care if you brush your teeth in the pee-tub! Get out of my sight!'

He jammed his pipe back in his mouth and got back behind his paper. Then I had the sense to let the argument drop and I seized my toothbrush and my record card and slunk off, red faced, to break the news to the teacher. She was standing anxiously at the schoolhouse door when I arrived.

'You've been a long time; is the baby all right?'

'Yes miss, he's fine . . .' and I proceeded to blurt out the whole story while she stood with her jaw muscle twitching as she struggled to keep her face straight.

'O well,' she said when I was finished. 'There's a good word for this kind of situation; it's *emergency*. I think this is an emergency which you and I can deal with without involving the *Crusaders' Own Paper.* You come in and I'll give you a spare cake of dentifrice and when you've brushed your teeth I'll certify your card.'

She was already sealing a large brown envelope when I came back from the washroom.

'There's another cake of dentifrice for your brother. You'd better tell him to keep it out of the baby's reach. Run away for your dinner now; I don't suppose having brushed your teeth *before* your meal will do you any harm for once!'

'Thank you, miss.' I muttered as I made for the door.

'O by the way . . .' She paused as I stood half-way through the doorway. 'I shouldn't say it, perhaps, but I think your essay is very good indeed. Very original.'

I raced off home thanking God and Washington Irving in turn.

Chapter Eleven

THE anatomy of cruelty is something that men will go on dissecting till the holocaust. What the city man will regard as cruelty in the country man, may be part of the essential fabric of survival for the latter – whether it be the killing of a fox to protect his flock or the cutting of a sheep's throat to provide food for his family. The latter is forbidden by law now for reasons of hygiene apart from anything else, although certain immigrant communities have it as a tenet of their religion that the animal to be eaten must be bled to death. The same people who devise these laws and are prepared to force them on minorities against the cherished beliefs of those minorities are, themselves, quite happy to don red jackets and follow hounds or sit in laboratories and refine the qualities of napalm. The computations of the contradictions are endless and, in support of an apparent cruelty, somebody will always find or invent a justification. One of the few *real* thrashings that I remember ever getting from my mother was for killing a baby rabbit. She hadn't been very happy about my keeping it in a cage anyway because, she assured me, it probably still required its mother's milk even although I had caught it while it was incautiously nibbling at some blades of grass in a corner from which it couldn't escape. But she let me try. For several days I kept trying to tempt the little thing with grass and cabbage leaves, and even tried to force some warm cow's milk down its throat; it was no good and, eventually, it became clear to me that the thing was dying. Instead of being sorry for it I became insanely angry with it, and I was in the process of hammering it to death with a kitchen shovel when my mother came round the corner and caught me. She didn't say a word. She picked the rabbit up and deftly threw its neck, took me into the house, lowered my trousers and belted me till I screamed. 'Let that be a lesson to you,' she said. 'And if I catch you being cruel to an animal again you'll get that three times over. She herself would wring a cockerel's neck without a thought or walk past a sheep being slaughtered without turning a hair. The difference is clear enough now, but it was a long time before it became clear to the young mind.

It never occurred to anybody that gin-trapping was cruel, and certainly it didn't for a moment occur to me even although the memory of the thrashing was still with me. Today I would unhesitatingly report anybody I found using a gin trap or anything resembling it, but then it was a legitimate part of the hunt and had all the primeval thrill of pitting cunning against cunning. The warrens in the sand-dunes made ferreting difficult because it was almost impossible to spot which were the bolt-holes, and one could fill in half a dozen and still leave one escape open. For the same reason, though to a lesser extent, trapping presented its own problems; by early winter even the youngest litters of the new season's crop of rabbits had their survival instincts honed to a fine degree, and the least disturbance at the mouth of a burrow, the tiniest trace of metal showing or the smell of sweaty hands was enough to make them divert to one of their 'back doors'; wily old bucks wouldn't even bother to do that, choosing instead to jump clean over the trap and hop back in over it again. There was nothing more humiliating than seeing the marks of their landing heavily imprinted at each end of the trap with the sand over the fangs of the gin trap undisturbed. My brother and I knew all that on the first evening that we set our dozen traps, and although it took us hours we eliminated every possible trace of our activities. The idea of the gin trap is devilishly simple. The hinged serrated jaws run through a hole in a strong spring which, when pressed down, allows the jaws to fall open; a simple catch drops over one of the jaws and is clipped into a notched flange on the edge of a two inch square 'tongue', and the upward pressure of the spring against the tongue and catch keeps one jaw open under pressure while the other flaps flat. When any pressure is put on the tongue it yields and releases the catch allowing the spring to snap the jaws viciously together. The first secret is to set the plate and the catch so finely that the faintest pressure releases the spring; the second secret is in the careful spreading of soil over the trap using the palm of the hand with the fingers spread wide so that if the trap springs accidentally the vicious teeth glide over the taut skin of the palm. Somebody with small hands has to be doubly careful.

The cruelty, of course, is that the animal caught by a foreleg is held there helplessly, because the trap is securely pegged into the ground at the end of a short chain. The beast caught on the way to his evening feed is held in agony all night long with its instinct telling it that death will come sooner or later; the more fortunate one is caught on his way to the dawn graze so he doesn't have to wait so long; the occasionally very fortunate one is the one who struggles so hard that he severs one of his legs and gets away to live on three.

We were up at the crack of dawn and raced each other down to the warrens. At the first trap we stopped in horror. It contained our ageing cat, Tiger. Had either of us been alone he would have cried. It wasn't in Tiger's nature to go hunting in winter, and going into rabbit burrows was certainly not the nature of his attack. He must have scented us and allowed his curiosity get the better of him. A strange cat in a rabbit trap can be ferociously dangerous; poor old Tiger's instinct must have told him that it was all a mistake, and he waited patiently while we released him. He was lucky that he was a strong-limbed brute and had chanced into an old trap in which the spring was weakening, so he got off with only broken skin and a very sore paw. The next ten traps were unsprung as we had left them. The last one contained a dogfish!

We gaped at each other in astonishment and total disbelief. We were two hundred yards from the sands, far less the sea – which was another quarter of a mile away. We knew that eels travelled overland, but they had never been known to molest anything. We knew that dogfish would eat anything, but nobody had ever heard of a dogfish leaving the sea of his own accord. We sat down to think it out. And when the truth dawned on us it was humiliating. Gillespie's mother had devised the fishing method of setting yards of long line with innumerable baited hooks stretched out along the sands when the tide was at its lowest, allowing the tide to come in and cover the line, and then – as soon as the tide had receded again – she would be down at the ebb to collect her catch before the sea-birds got it. It was a primitive form of fishing, but it worked. The only trouble was that our coast was swarming with dogfish which either took the bait themselves or else took a goodly proportion of the fish that she had caught. She must have been down at her lines at first light, and the dogfish was her way of saying that our technique was so amateur that even a casual passer-by could spot our traps. And if she could, what chance did we have against wily rabbits? We went home bitterly ashamed, and when we told my father he laughed his head off!

Had we found 12 unsprung traps we might have given up in disgust, but being made to look foolish made us even more determined and we decided to go back that evening and re-set all our dozen gin traps; in our chagrin we hadn't even bothered to re-spring the two that had been so humiliatingly closed. And when we did go back, to our joy three of our traps from the night before had three fat rabbits in them – two three-quarter grown ones, and a buck with a neck like leather.

From them on we never looked back. We set our traps night and morning, except Saturday nights and Sundays, and we had rabbit meat and to spare. But a new factor emerged, significant yet again of the fact that, although we didn't know it, the 'slump' as it was called in those days was on the turn. Various firms began to advertise for rabbit skins, notably one in Appleby, offering tuppence a skin plus the cost of postage. The skin had to be removed whole and uncut, head and all, all the tallow removed from it, and hung up by the nose to dry till it was crispy hard. Before long we were despatching bundles of three dozen skins a week and postal orders for six shillings began arriving in addition to the dole. And then advertisements for whelks began to appear. It was a cold, weary job collecting whelks from the rock-pools; it was too cold and wet for us as children, but our parents went at it like people who had found gold, and all along the road by the sea-shore piles of bags of whelks began to appear for the market in a place called Billingsgate. Whenever I see a stall on the pavement selling whelks in Soho I make a point of buying a packet and a pin for old times' sake, because it was thanks to rabbit skins and whelks sold in far off, unheard of places, that I got my pair of winter boots that year.

Then, for the umpteenth time, my father announced that he was going to get a loom, and the usual argument ensued.

'A loom? Now, of all times? You must be out of your mind. What use is a loom to you when the house is stacked with unsold tweeds?' My mother was well accustomed to this old aspiration of my father's. 'And anyway you can't weave.'

'I was talking to my father when I was in Tarbert last week, and he knows somebody who's selling a loom and would be willing to wait for payment. He's coming down for a few days next week to teach me. I think times are getting better. They're even saying that there's going to be a Harris Tweed stall at the Empire Exhibition in Glasgow, and a competition for the best weaver.'

'And you'll be winning it?'

'I wouldn't be surprised!'

My mother dropped the subject; she was learning not to rise to what she manifestly regarded as his off-beat sense of humour.

'And where are you putting this wonderful loom that's going to weave us gold? In the bedroom with us and four children?' She glanced hastily in the direction of my brother and myself, but she needn't have bothered. We had overheard one of the village women teasing her with some of the crude, spicey, humour that always accompanied references to pregnancy, and we even knew that the new arrival was only a couple of weeks away.

Father had obviously put a lot of thought into this latest scheme of his without mentioning it to anyone, probably because he knew that most people would laugh him out of court for going into the weaving business when the Harris Tweed market was as stagnant as a pool left behind by a summer high tide. He had arranged to get some corrugated iron from somewhere and, although she didn't know it, my mother's own brother – the ship's carpenter with Sopwith – was home on holiday and had agreed to come and put up a lean-to hut against the rear of our little house. Like all Sopwith's crewmen he was very much a local hero; although *Endeavour 11* had failed ingloriously in her challenge for the America's Cup she had caused a sensation and earned herself yards of breathtaking press publicity by breaking her tow with *Philante* on her homeward journey, losing all communication for days on end, and finally making immaculate landfall in Ireland. Visits by Uncle Alex and Wee Grandfather in the same winter were highlights, and listening to grown-up conversation late into the night one began to get a feeling that better times were ahead. My father wasn't the only person in the village who was optimistic. The last of our bachelor ex-servicemen had, to everybody's surprise, by-passed the traditional system of building himself a temporary house and had gone straight ahead with a beautiful stone and lime one instead.

The loom was to represent a major change in our lives. Where my father had been lacking in enthusiasm for the croft, and had seen it only as a place of living, not a *way* of living, he found in the loom a chance to express himself; and perhaps it's not too fanciful to think that it allowed him express the poetry that was undoubtedly in him, and which would have found its expression in writing had he been born in another place or even two generations later on. He believed that when the market did revive there would be a demand for genuine Harris Tweed (already mill-spun yarn was creeping into such tweeds as were being made, and there were rumours that 'Harris Tweed' was even being made in Japan) and also that there was a need for greater innovation. There was a tendency to stick to traditional designs and colours; even although synthetic dyes were fast pushing out the more laborious and time-consuming natural dyes, there was still an inclination to cling to the simplest and best tried colour schemes like crotal and white.

Not that crotal and white was as humdrum as a simple

definition of it as 'brown and white' implies. Crotal was the grey lichen which, over hundreds of years, had grown over the moorland rocks particularly; it seemed to get a better hold in the dry moor air than down in the moister atmosphere of the coastal crofts. Or it may be, of course, that, over generations, the nearer rocks had been scraped clean and that years enough hadn't passed for the crotal to renew itself. In the summer it ripened and, at the same time as the wool began to rise from the sheep ready for shearing, the grey crotal eased itself off the mother rock. That was when the women went for it, equipped only with an old soup spoon off which one corner had been filed to leave it with a scraping edge and a sharp point to get into the crevices – because crotal was scarce enough to make it prudent to scrape each rock clean. In a long day, punctuated only by a picnic meal, two women could fill a sizeable sack; one woman could carry it because the best crotal was as light as down. When the shearing was done and the new fleeces brought home, a dry summer day would be chosen for the first dyeing day. Each croft wife had a huge three legged pot, capable of taking two or three fleeces, and all year round it sat outside beside a crude little rectangle of stones scorched black over the years. On the day, a peat fire would be lit in the stones, and the big pot filled. First a layer of washed fleece, then a good thick sprinkling of crotal, another layer of fleece and another layer of crotal and so on, tier upon tier, till the pot was almost full, leaving just room for water. The whole cauldron was then boiled for several hours with the addition of only extra water to keep it from boiling dry and one handful of common sorrel to fasten the dye. At the end of the day the fleeces were a rich dark red and they were tipped into the river for the flowing water to take away waste red liquid and the lichen which was now bleached white, having surrendered its colour.

You could tell that it was dyeing day in a village long before you came in sight of the houses. The open air peat fires added their stronger aroma to the peat smell that hung heavy from the domestic fires anyway. But the boiling crotal, marrying with the wool, added its own peculiar tartness; it was a smell that lingered in the nostrils, lingered unmistakably in the tweed into which the crotal wool would be woven, into the distant future when the tweed itself wore out; it was a smell that still lingers in the memory of any Harrisman born before the 1930s. Since the war most of the crotal on the rocks has been left to grow in peace, and, here and there, rocks that were scraped clean by women long since forgotten are beginning to grow a crop that will never be disturbed by an old kitchen spoon.

But it wasn't the smell alone. There was also the sight. Through the villages, during the drying days of summer and autumn, the dry-stone dykes and the modern new fences were draped with fleeces of many colours, for the range of dyes that centuries of expertise had imagined out of every sprig of vegetable matter spanned far beyond the rainbow. But, without question, the shades that drew the eye because of their preponderance were the dark red of the crotal and the one that wasn't a colour at all, the pure white. The white it was that had married with the lichen to make the crotal colour; they would intertwine again to produce many combinations. A handful of crotal-dyed wool teased in among a lot of white would give a light oatmeal colour; a stronger addition of crotal would give a richer brown. And then, of course, as spun threads they would be brought together in the loom according to the tweed-maker's design – two by two brown and white, dog-tooth brown and white, or the one checked or double-checked on the other. It didn't matter what the combination, the general name was still 'crotal and white', and the variations on the theme could be as diverse as whim; its shades as light or dark as thought. Just as the taste of crowdie and cream has been for me the lingering taste of the bitter-sweet of childhood, so the very word tweed evokes the phrase *crotal and white* and it, in turn, evokes the memory of the year we got the loom, and the year that things began to get better.

I think my mother really began to believe that things were on the mend when she sold her first tweed in many months, just shortly after her fourth boy was born. It was as if Providence had at last stepped in to ease a burden that was becoming too heavy. My father's pleasure in the loom was having an enlightening effect on the whole household; he hadn't yet actually started weaving full lengths of tweed on it, there was a big enough stockpile in the house to keep us going even if the market surged instead of just beginning slowly to gain momentum. So he spent his time practising and experimenting with patterns, and when he wasn't at the loom he was his old good-humoured self again. Perhaps the fact that he now seemed to be able to afford a regular supply of tobacco for his pipe had something to do with it, or perhaps the fact that he was able to resume getting his daily paper again. A regular daily bus service from Stornoway had started to challenge our own thrice weekly one, and the Stornoway bus had begun delivering papers. 'Delivering' is, perhaps, a slightly sophisticated word for the system; what happened, in fact, was that the driver rolled up the paper and without as much as touching his brake flung it out of the bus door as he passed each client's house.

The *Daily Record* had stepped up its challenge to the *Daily Express*, but the villagers' response – frequently influenced by the demands of the younger members of the family – was to agree on which household was to get which paper and then swop them round next day. Thus the adults got the benefit of the different news angles and the *Daily Record*'s strip cartoons, while the younger ones, who were still loyal to Rupert Bear, were able to keep track of their tartan-trousered hero. Rupert's trousers haven't changed over the years although he has lost out on column inches, and my memory of those days still makes me think of them as tartan although sense tells me now that they're check. When the *Express* moves into greater areas of colour they may turn out to be crotal and white, who knows?

As far as I was concerned, the *Daily Express* had the edge on its rival for a totally different reason. It had begun to serialize stories and, occasionally, books. It was there that I made my first acquaintance with A. J. Cronin's novels, such as *The Citadel*, although I would have to search that journal's files to find the year. But I know that it was in the year of the run-up to my bursary examination (the turning point of my life) that the daily paper became a bone of contention between my father and myself. I was under instructions from him to read the paper from cover to cover because, he maintained, while it might not be great literature it was a goldmine of background information which I might be able to put to advantage in my test papers; and I was, he kept assuring me, 'reading history as it was being made' – because he was convinced that we were now coming up to a war. Mussolini had paid a State Visit to Hitler, and father's reading of events was that the three dictators, Hitler, Mussolini and Franco would carve up Europe between them and then swallow up Russia before beginning to swallow up each other. 'It will be the Roman Empire all over again,' he maintained. 'Europe will be one huge empire and then become too big for itself and begin to fall apart!' I was inclined to believe anything he had to say that concerned the Roman Empire, no matter how indirectly, because, by now, I was convinced that he knew Gibbon off by heart in much the same way as he had managed to coax me into learning off by heart a substantial portion of Macaulay's *Lays of Ancient Rome*. Not that that was any hardship. Mamilius and Herminius were more exciting antagonists by far than David and Goliath, and Horatius left Joshua right out in the cold.

But it was becoming noticeable to me that my father's enthusiasm for me to read the paper was always in inverse proportion to the degree of interest he happened to have in it himself. If I hadn't been able to get my hands on the paper by the time he came in from the loom, then it would suddenly become much more important that I should study my formal school books than that I should waste time on the paper 'which hasn't got much fresh to say for itself these days'.

Matters came to a head over one particular serial, the name of which I can't even now remember. But I do remember that it finished each day on a cliff-hanger and I could barely concentrate on anything else in or out of school till I got home and laid hands on the *Daily Express*. That is unless my father laid his hands on it first. Although he kept protesting that it was a poor look-out for me if I got so involved in a piece of cheap fiction that it occupied time when I should be concentrating on my preparations for the bursary, it was patently obvious that he himself was prepared to slip in from the loom as soon as the rattle of the Stornoway bus passing the gate indicated that the paper had arrived. And it was equally obvious that, unusually for him, he skipped hastily over the news on Page One and sat with his pipe clenched in his teeth and his jaw muscle twitching as he ploughed stolidly through Pages Six and Seven, which were the double-page spread of the story.

The plot was so simple that I remember it clearly although I have long since forgotten the twists and turns of it. It was about a man who had fallen off a liner in the middle of the Pacific Ocean at an early hour of the dawn and his absence hadn't been noticed till night. The liner put round immediately of course, but from the beginning, it seemed fairly obvious that it was going to be touch and go, but that, by dint of brilliant navigation and with a large element of good luck, the man would be found just before a shark got him or else he went down for the third and last time. I had begun to figure out the mechanisms of the suspense story.

But this one turned differently. Attention barely focused on the liner at all. Instead of that we stayed with the man. As soon as he had hit the water and failed to make his cries for help heard, he worked it out for himself that his safety lay in keeping calm and keeping afloat. Just that. Keeping afloat. He was a powerful swimmer but he knew that any exertion would be worse than futile; any movement on his part would not only drain his energy but take him further from the place where the liner would ultimately come to search for him. And so he kicked off his shoes and just floated for hour after hour after hour.

The hours spread into a couple of days and, of course, they spread over many days in the *Daily Express*. The man's life, in time-honoured tradition, floated slowly through his mind as his hope began to fade. Everything, good or bad, that he had done drifted through his failing consciousness because heat and thirst and sheer immersion were taking their toll. The climax, as far as the *Daily Express* was concerned, came on Saturday, with the last episode; but whatever agonies of suspense were being suffered by mainland readers they were multiplied for us because, despite the improved delivery of the bus, we still didn't get the daily paper till the day after publication. And, of course, we didn't get Saturday's paper till Monday. On Monday it was touch and go whether the bus arrived a few minutes before or a few minutes after school was dismissed and I sat through the Monday afternoon unable to concentrate on anything going on around me, wondering about the fate of the man in the middle of the Pacific. The bus passed me on my way home from school and I could see my father walking smartly down to the gate and practically catching the paper in its flight like a cricketer in the slips. I knew there was no point in hurrying. By the time I got into the house he was propped in his favourite position at the head of the table, with his back jammed against the corner of the table and the wall, with his feet up against the edge of the big cupboard. I sat on St Clement's bench and waited.

At long last he handed over the paper with a smile, lit his pipe and puffed patiently away at it watching my every reaction. And I must have gone through the gamut. The suspense was magnificently built up; the man reached one agony of despair in the penultimate line, then jack-knifed and sank.

I was stunned. I had been convinced that he would be rescued. But there it was in large letters, THE END. I put the paper down and became aware of my father looking over at me and smiling quizzically.

'Bit disappointing isn't it?'

'Disappointing!' I couldn't believe I was hearing him properly. 'Disappointing? You mean that he wasn't saved?'

'No. That it turned out to be such a bad story.'

'A bad story!' I felt angry on behalf of the man, the *Daily Express* and myself. 'It was a great story – it got more exciting every day right up to the end. It was one of the best stories I've ever read!'

He reached across for the paper and folded it back to Page One. 'You're forgetting something; really great fiction is stuff which a man invents but which could just be true.'

'But that could be true . . . every word of it. How do you think it couldn't?'

'Just tell me this, then. If he was all alone there all those days, with nobody to talk to and nobody to know even how he died, how could they know what he was thinking just before he went down?'

I felt utterly deflated, and considerably let down. Angry with myself too that I hadn't worked that out for myself. I got up to go outside, and just as I reached the door I remembered something.

'Will you explain something to me then?'

'Yes. What?' He was just drifting into his paper.

'If they couldn't know what that man was thinking, how could they know what that woman was dreaming during the French Revolution when she dropped dead in her sleep when her maid tapped her neck with her fan during her dream?'

The muscle in his jaw twitched. But I could see him squeezing a smile back as he lifted up the *Daily Express* between us.

'O that!' he said. 'O that was different!'

I didn't pursue the argument, but I knew that for the first time the round had gone to me. And in every story I've ever written I've tried to make the plot at the very least such that 'it could just be true'!

Chapter Twelve

NATIONS and people aren't aware of pulling out of national Depressions and Recessions in one purposeful surge from a state of 'all's ill' to a glorious realization of 'all's well', no matter how much pundits interpret symptoms for them. It doesn't happen that way, any more than the man who is recovering from a long and weary illness suddenly sits up one day and says, 'Yesterday I was ill and dying; today, hallelujah, I am fit and well.' The only reason why we, in our new village, were aware of the recovery of the thirties probably more sharply than most of the rest of the kingdom was because a whole avalanche of progress and novelty overwhelmed us in a very short space of time. We were on the periphery of modernization in the early thirties, still without regular public transport, without electricity or gas, without running water in the vast majority of our homes, with 82 per cent of the population around us still suffering from tuberculosis, with no radio and with only the most rudimentary telephone service. Having advanced so little we couldn't slip back so very far, and what we were missing most were luxuries and conveniences to which we had barely had time to become accustomed. We had had, after all, a major local slump of our own in the mid-twenties when Lord Leverhulme's great plans for the industrialization of Harris had collapsed overnight, and all that remained of them now was the decaying town of Leverburgh – named after the great magnate.

When the world and the nearest bit of it to us, the mainland, began to pull out of the Depression, the effects of the mainland recovery had no immediate impact on us; but when it began to have, it began to have it very noticeably. When the cities could again afford fish, the fishing of the Northlands boomed; when the cities began to afford luxuries again and when the nation began to export, the Harris Tweed industry boomed: it is an industry that collapsed and boomed very rapidly in those days, and because it was so cottage-based its fluctuations were felt immediately. And then, within the space of a couple of years, radio, the aeroplane, daily bus service, mobile vans, and people to teach us how to make the most of life all began to descend on us at the same time. The markets of the south were obviously bursting at the seams and Calum the Post's van began to sag on its springs under the weight of advertising that poured in on our newly discovered land. Even the margarine companies convinced themselves that there was a market in a part of the world where every house had at least one cow, and most frequently two, and an unending supply of free fresh butter. The remarkable thing was that the margarine companies had spectacular success, not because people particularly liked their products but because people liked the varieties of gifts and bonuses that they were prepared to dish out in a bid to cut each others' throats and profits.

It was a matter of puzzlement and, indeed envy, for my own family when the last of the ex-servicemen forged ahead and built his new stone house leaving us standing – by now the only one of the temporary shacks that hadn't been replaced. It was beginning to rankle with me as a boy. I was beginning to feel that my father had somehow let us down, as we became more and more overcrowded in our tiny two rooms without amenity of any kind; and yet here was a bachelor, without any family at all, moving into his spacious new house. Many years later when he was on his death-bed I was able to put the question to that one-time bachelor who was, by then, widowed and being looked after by a devoted family.

'Was my father a bad crofter?' I asked him.

There is nobody as skilled as the Hebridean at the gentle answer that turneth away hurt.

'Your father was a very good neighbour,' he replied.

'But am I right in thinking he wasn't a very good crofter?'

'He was very well liked in this village.'

Finally I decided to try the blunt approach.

'Tell me then, how were you able to build this nice home while we never got out of the temporary house?'

'Ah well, you see, you needed a bit of capital even with the grants and loans, and your father wasn't able to accumulate the capital.'

'But what about you? How did you manage to accumulate capital? You didn't even have a loom except for a very short time.'

'Ah but I won that competition!'

I didn't know what he was talking about.

'What competition was that?'

'The margarine company, don't you remember? You had to buy a half pound of margarine with a wee coupon on the wrapper. And you had to complete a slogan which began *A pound of Echo margarine is equal to* . . . in less than six words. Ach, people were putting in all sorts of daft things, but I just put in *equal to a pound of butter* (God help me, I didn't even like margarine!) and I won a hundred pounds. That was a lot of money in those days. . . .'

It certainly was. About a third of the total price of a new house with an upstairs and a bathroom out of the cold!

That sort of luck didn't come our way, but a lot of good fortune did. My father decided early on that the shape of the Harris Tweed trade as a cottage industry must be re-thought if it was to survive as the sort of industry he felt it should be – a small domestic craft producing a very high quality of material, not so much in the vast rolls of before but as short suit and costume lengths for the tourists who were then beginning to discover us in their hundreds as their own financial circumstances in the cities and in the stockbroker belts improved. We represented adventure. Primitive people living in primitive conditions speaking a 'foreign' language, and with a great aura of romance surrounding us. Some were tempted to come and see 'the people living in poverty in poor hovels strung out along the roadside' that Louis MacNeice had written about in *I crossed the Minch*. Many more were being lured by the romantic world that had been portrayed for over a hundred years in the writings of Sir Walter Scott, and perpetuated by people like Marjorie Kennedy Fraser whose harp-accompanied "Songs of the Hebrides" were the rage in the salons of London. It was a far cry from six sweating women thumping a heavy soggy tweed – soaked in mature urine – on a wooden trestle, accompanied by their own rather raucous singing, to the elegance of a gowned lady singing a polished version of that same tune in the drawing room of Londonderry House. But no matter. Those who were tempted to search out the country of origin of the songs couldn't be disappointed. Either they saw the red sunsets and heard the fairy songs and went away happy, or they saw what was 'primitive poverty' by their standards and their pleasure was not the less sweet for being vicarious.

Those who went to the trouble of calling on us and meeting us were, without exception, extremely nice people. I remember only one case of offence being given and taken unwittingly, and that was over the head of me. I was seated at the end of the table reading a book one day when two English ladies arrived and were invited in by my mother. They tried to engage me in conversation and I was singularly and unusually unwilling to respond. I kept my head buried in my book and they weren't to notice that I wasn't turning the pages because the book was in fact a complete shielding of a deep resentment of my own which my mother was either unwilling or unable to explain. Three months earlier the *Crusaders' Own Paper* had announced that the response to their competition for an article on "The Place Where I Live" had been so sensationally large that the editor had decided in his wisdom to award three prizes and that, in time-honoured fashion, they would print the third-prize winner's composition first and announce his prize – which would reach him along with the issue carrying his article – and meantime would we all continue polishing our *Ivory Castles* with Gibb's dentifrice while we were grinding them with excitement? The anticipation was acute. The third-prize winner had written about life in some part of London of which we had never heard, but I was glad I hadn't won the prize because it was some Encyclopaedia or other, and I had set my heart on a bicycle. A month later the second prize was announced and the article it was won with was published, but I haven't the vaguest recollection where the winner came from or what the prize was – except that it wasn't a bicycle. And then came the day of the first prize, and when the teacher walked into the class-room I didn't have to be told. The beam on her face said everything. Not only had I won, but I'd received exceptional commendation and my piece was given what a newspaperman would call a Page One lead – its title and my first by-line splurged right across the page under the mast-head of the paper itself. But what was this? What was the box the teacher was holding in her hand? I was summoned out to stand in front of the class to listen to a speech praising me in terms that I had never heard before, and only half heard then, because I knew that whatever that box held it did not contain a bicycle, and my best guess was a wrist-watch – which I didn't own and didn't particularly want. I hadn't been given time to read the editor's commendation before being summoned out to the teacher's desk, but one or two of my class-mates had been reading it while the teacher had been speaking and I could see broad smirks appearing on their faces. At last I was allowed to rip the parcel open, and then the rather beautiful presentation box inside sprang apart at the press of a button to show, nestling on a bed of velvet, a thing called a *Chromatic Harmonica* or what was, by the only name that I knew for it, a very large and very elaborate mouth-organ of the type that Mr Larry Adler had almost certainly not yet aspired to. Even if Miss Ethel Bassin hadn't so definitely put my musicianship into such negative perspective I would have known that not in a hundred years could I have mastered that monstrosity with a sprung button at the end of it for changing keys, which I couldn't even hear far less play. That had been yesterday, and I hadn't spoken to anybody since.

'I think that boy's a bookworm,' one of the lady tourists had remarked as she left and my mother had flushed scarlet. She might have been saving up her wrath to give me a row for my rudeness as soon as the visitors left, but that saved my skin. Nobody was going to call her eldest son a worm. The visitors must have wondered why their hostess had suddenly turned so chilly as they left, just as I was left to wonder why she had suddenly become so charming and affectionate to me. I have no idea where that musical monstrosity went; to her eternal credit the teacher never even referred to it again.

Our little house had suddenly become a mecca for tourists who came to bathe on our white beaches. My father had become a very proficient weaver, and his policy of weaving short suit lengths was paying off. He loved company, and when the tourists arrived he would spend as much time as they cared to spare – regardless of the possibilities of a sale – instructing them in the subtleties of creating the dyes from various plants; he had a little pan on a paraffin stove on which he could demonstrate the dyeing of crotal. He would then show them how a tweed was 'framed' to decide the lay-out and design of the warp (the longways threads) and demonstrate how the shuttle carried the woof across to create the ultimate pattern or sett. His loom was one of the newer, heavy, kind known, appropriately, as *the big loom* and the operation of it was a very complicated business. Its four long wooden pedals had to be depressed and released in a pre-ordained order and with metronomic precision so that the warp was open when the weaver's beam was thrust furthest away with the left hand, to let the right hand fire the shuttle carrying the woof through the parted threads just a split second before the beam was thudded forwards towards the weaver to ram the cross threads into position. And then one foot moved the next appropriate pedal to lock the cross thread into place. It sounds complicated. It was. It was an operation which required split-second timing and perfect co-ordination between feet and hands, with each of the four limbs operating entirely independently of each other. But when the good weaver got into his rhythm, the shuttle clacked and the beam thudded in perfect harmony and with astonishing speed, and you could see the cloth growing inch by inch.

My father was a good weaver by any standards but, what was sometimes even more important on such occasions, he was an inveterate showman and his demonstrations were carried out to a running commentary which beguiled his watchers as a conjurer's patter disguises his sleight of hand. And then he would get off his narrow wooden seat.

'There's nothing to it as you can see. Here, weave a yard or two yourself and you'll be able to tell your friends that you're wearing a tweed that you wove yourself!' The unsuspecting tourist, who up to that point probably hadn't had the faintest intention of buying any tweed, would slip self-consciously on to the seat and proceed to get into a tangle of thread and machinery out of which Houdini couldn't have extricated himself, and in the end he, or she, would admit defeat in confusion – reduced to a nervous apologetic wreck in the case of a man, and to a giggling, blushing St Trinianite in the case of a woman.

'Would you like a wee shot at the wife's spinning wheel?' father would ask innocently.

'O Lord, no thanks! The time has flown and we simply must get back to – er – get back. . . . It's been a marvellous experience. Will your loom be all right?'

'Och probably! Don't you worry about that.'

Father always escorted them courteously down to the main road, and if there happened to be a sheep around he'd remark, 'That could well be the sheep that provided the wool for your tweed,' and the tourists could be seen to be storing up another piece of lore for recitation in the pub or the club back home. Father never stated that it *was* the sheep, only that it *could* be; nor did he have time to add that the sheep which had originally worn the wool could equally well be roaming the mountain tops two miles up, or have been eaten last winter.

The tourist industry can be a dangerous area of social economy, and there is an element of truth in the Highland argument that it can change a country into a nation of waiters. But we were fortunate in the calibre of person who came along in those pre-war days. Sometimes they never bought tweed. And nobody minded. By and large the people who came our way were professional people (whether they were initially attracted by the romantic idea or by curiosity) and with many of them my parents forged friendships that were to last for a lifetime. Some of them came back from time to time; many of them never returned again, probably because they had enjoyed the one holiday of a lifetime and couldn't afford the trip a second time. A substantial number kept up a correspondence for years, and sometimes we wouldn't hear from them except when a present arrived at Christmastime and their cards went to make Calum the Post's job harder. Some kept my father supplied with books, which he appreciated more than anything else.

The subtler influence which they exercised on us younger ones was much more far-reaching. As I've suggested throughout these pages the whole education system in our little 13-pupil school was geared to wean us away from our own culture and our own traditions. Our whole teaching was conducted in English and we could be punished for talking Gaelic in the playground. It was always stressed, in school and at home, that success meant qualifying to get away to College or University, or at the very least to a mainland job. Boys in particular were deemed to be failures if they left school at the age of fourteen (as they had to if they didn't pass the highly selective bursary examination) and became crofters or weavers or employees of some humble branch of Local Authority on their own home ground. To be a bus driver or a policeman or a commercial traveller in Glasgow carried a subtle social cachet, and more so if the person plying one or other of those trades got as far as Manchester or London. When such a person came home for a fortnight's holiday in summer he was rarely expected to give a helping hand with peat or with harvest; he was a gentleman, and invariably had pound notes to prove it. The tourists, unbeknown to themselves, were recruiting agents for those foreign fields – living examples of what we might hope to become if we worked at our books and 'got away'. When, belatedly, various organizations began to realize that we had a language and a culture worth preserving they began sending representatives round exhorting us to 'keep our language alive' and enlisting us in organizations for which we had to take solemn oaths promising 'to be a true Highlander as long as I live'. Up to that point we hadn't even been aware that our language was in danger of dying; we were merely learning an extra and more useful one. Nor were we aware that, as Highlanders, we were an endangered species. The effect of good intention was counter-productive and, not only were we now being encouraged to go away for the valid

143

purposes of education, but we were creatures from the reservation being treated as special cases like other aboriginal tribes who rubbed noses and did things civilized people regarded as quaint.

Although the last holiday at Big Grandfather's had not been an unqualified success, it had given a new zest to the idea of 'getting away'. To go to school in a village of three hundred people with thirteen shops, a bank, two churches, a pier where ships came and went, was as alluring a prospect as London has been for people from all over Britain through the ages. The idea of attending a school where each class was as big as our entire village school was a bit daunting, but the thought of being taught new subjects by men was very challenging and promising. There was only one way of getting there and that was by winning the bursary. I don't know how many bursaries were available in the whole county of Inverness-shire but not more than half a dozen pupils could hope to win bursaries out of the whole of the Southlands, in which there were some ten or eleven schools. The standard of teaching and the parental outlook in some of those villages was such that some schools would not present candidates at all, but we were extremely fortunate in having a zealous teacher who could be depended on to present at least one pupil every year. I was in the crop of pupils who had come almost through the whole of our school lives, apart from the first disastrous year, with herself, and she was now preparing to put forward four of us to compete. Only two of us could possibly hope to win a bursary but two of us, including me, were young enough to have a second chance next year if we failed; but by then others would have caught up with us and the competition would be just as strong.

I was by now totally committed to winning. Various little successes, like the *Crusaders'* composition, had given me a certain confidence in myself. The subjects we had to compete in were English, Geography, History, and Arithmetic, with the accent very heavily on English – which was sub-divided into Essay, Interpretation and Parsing. I had a fair confidence in myself but I decided that a little help from the Divinity would not go amiss and so, each morning and evening for the

144

three months before the examination, I crept away to a quiet corner on my own and prayed. It was a very simple prayer which varied very little, but one sentence that didn't change one syllable was the sentence, 'Please God help me to win the bursary.' And I was pretty certain that He would!

The examination was scheduled to take place in May in the large school (large by our standards) of Leverburgh, five miles away. This was to be my first visit to Leverburgh, and it was decided that my father would walk down with me the evening before and that we would both stay in the house of a far-out relative of his very near to the school so that nothing could possibly prevent me getting to my desk in time in the morning. For the very first time ever it was decided that I should have a bought suit and new pair of low cut sandal type shoes. I suspect that at the back of the parental minds was the thought that both suit and shoes would be suitable for the great day – when it came – when I should be leaving home to go to the Northlands to school; when, in effect, I would be leaving home for ever and be returning only as one of the stylish holiday visitors that we had come to envy.

We set off, my father and myself, in time to arrive at our host's house not too late for an evening meal. It was a beautiful evening, and as we walked past the school and the old manse and the graveyard I felt strangely lonely and a little sad. I remembered the night that Gillespie and I had stolen out of the house when we were supposed to be sound asleep and made our ways to the feast before the wedding of Mary and James. It was broad daylight now, but that night there had been a fat moon save in the dark shadow of the churchyard where fear had all but turned us back; and if it had we would have missed a rare old ceremony which I, certainly, would never have had the chance to see again. This was to be the parting of the ways for Gillespie and myself. He and his parents had decided that he would stay on at the village school till he was fourteen and then take the mainland trail in search of a job. Jobs were becoming easy to get in Glasgow, with the fear of war growing and preliminary preparations being made even although noises from London indicated that there was going to be peace in our time.

I could sense that my father was nervous himself. He chattered inconsequentially instead of trying to involve me in any of the discussions that he liked to lead me into with the sole purpose, I was beginning to realize, of passing on to me as much information as he had collected on his own way through life. This wasn't his eldest son going to sit this crucial examination; this was his alter ego. This was the young himself getting a chance in life, or else somebody representing his old self getting the chance that he had never had; it was perhaps the justification of what he had fought for, those four years in France – the chance of a new beginning for a new generation. The only reference he made to the future was the often repeated assertion that if he had his life to live again he would go to University and study English and be a journalist, and I knew that he had been trying to edge me in that direction from the age that I could even begin to comprehend – never with pressure, but with an influence much subtler than that. Strangely enough he didn't seem to take into consideration at all that once I had made the breach I would come into contact with other influences – in Tarbert School itself, in High School and in University.

The evening passed quickly in the company of a boy a year or two older than myself, who attended the school in which I was going to sit my exam. He took me down to show me the building, and I was overwhelmed by its size. It was only four or five rooms in fact, but huge by the standards of our little village school.

It felt even bigger next morning at nine o'clock as fifteen of us met – total strangers to each other apart from the four of us from my own school – and we were placed in single desks spaced far apart from each other under the eagle eye of an invigilating minister, who started off the morning with prayer, followed by a little homily on honesty, and then a rapid recitation of the elementary examination rules. 'There's a clock on the wall,' he said. 'It's probably the most important thing in the room. You must attempt to pace yourselves so that you answer every question and not just get bogged down in a long-winded answer to one question that you happen to find easy.' It was my very first experience of formal examination conditions, but there I was at no disadvantage compared with the rest. I remember distinctly writing my name and age, school and address, and then nothing else at all. The most important day of my life was over before I was fully aware that it had begun.

We had to report to our own school next morning so that the teacher could satisfy her own curiosity as to how we had done, but whatever conclusions she came to she kept to herself. We were given the rest of the day off as a special treat, but life seemed strangely empty and there seemed to be little point in having a day off with my brother and Gillespie at school.

It would be the middle of August before we would get the official results, but I didn't have to wait that long. In mid-July (the first July that I had not been at Big Grandfather's) a car drew up at the gate and a highly respected minister from a village south of us came out of it and was making his way to the house, when he noticed my father working in the stackyard – clearing it out and preparing it to dry out for the new harvest in September or October. Mother and I were curious to know why the minister had called and mother, noticing that he had made a point of ignoring the house and walking straight to my father in the stackyard, was convinced that it was some bad news connected with her family in the Northlands that the minister wanted to pass on to my father first. But after a little while he left, smiling and raising his hat to mother as he passed the window; and from the fact that father didn't come rushing in as soon as the minister's back was turned we concluded that, whatever the reason for the minister's call, it had been of minor importance. Or perhaps he had just called for a quick chat having noticed father in the stackyard; they had been close friends when they had both been young men, and before the dog collar had separated their stations.

As soon as the minister's car was out of sight father did come rushing in, and from the light in his eye and the smile on his face it was obvious that the minister had certainly not been the bearer of bad news. For the first time in his life my father walked over to me with his hand held out. 'Congratulations, my boy,' he said. 'You've done it; I knew you would! You've won the bursary!' And mother began to cry.

'But not a word to anybody, not even to your own young brother. The minister was on his way back from a meeting of the Education Committee in Inverness, and he was really breaking faith by telling us at all. But he knew how anxious we were. Not a word to anybody. It won't be easy, but you'll have to keep quiet till the official letter comes.'

After that the next three weeks passed like one week. Mother got her catalogues out and she and father began planning what they could afford in the way of wardrobe. I don't suppose I had ever been so helpful around the croft in my life, partly to show some kind of gratitude, partly to keep myself busy so as to avoid the temptation to tell Gillespie the news. But just as I had remembered to pray for success, I now remembered to say 'Thank you', and night and morning I thanked God for helping me to win the bursary.

As it drew near to the middle of August father made a point of staying back from Calum the Post's van and letting me go down to collect the mail myself. At last it arrived, and Calum twinkled as he handed it to me. 'There you are,' he said, 'I thought you'd be passing out on me with excitement. I'll call in on my way back and hear all about it!' It was Saturday, the only day on which Calum returned home after completing his delivery; normally he spent the night in lodgings at the far end of his run and did the southward trip in the morning collecting the mail.

I rushed into the living room where my father and mother were standing waiting with smiles on their faces. 'Open it yourself,' my father said. 'It's your life it's about after all.' I ripped the envelope open and read without thinking and without taking in what I was saying. There were only two lines, but they were like an epitaph.

We very much regret to inform you that you have not been successful in your application for a bursary.

My mother began to cry softly. But I couldn't.

Chapter Thirteen

'NEVER mind boy,' said my father forcing a smile, 'you've got another chance and that's the most important thing to have in life. I should never have told you something that was told me in confidence. And I should have known better than to believe a minister. . . .'

'John!'

That sort of remark never failed to snap my mother out of whatever kind of mood she was in; she was too good a woman to regard herself as being religious, but she certainly didn't subscribe to my father's belief that God didn't mind his leg being pulled and that it was 'the sanctimonious buggers he objected to!'

'It's perfectly true. Ministers are only like wirelesses; it's only when they're in the pulpit that they've got their aerials plugged in; for the rest of the time they're just full of interference!'

'I'm not going to listen to any more of this!' She snatched the kettle off the stove and proceeded to fill it although we had just had a cup of tea before Calum the Post had come; it was her automatic escape route from an uncomfortable corner. 'In any case, I thought you had a tweed to finish!'

'Ach you're quite right as usual.' He turned to pick his pipe off the mantelpiece. 'And perhaps Finlay will go and catch us that fry of brown trout he's been promising us. Eh?'

That was calculated to jerk me out of my depression. I had come back from the Northlands that last summer boasting about the number of brown trout my cousin and I had caught during the holidays; it was the annual recitative and never a

whit more inhibited by the truth than that of more sophisticated fishermen. My father's jibe was more than justified,
however; whatever modicum of success I might have had on
the lochs of the Northlands I had never caught one single
trout on the teeming lochs of the southern moors. And God
knows I had thrashed them the previous summer in my own
private obsession with keeping away from any road or track
that might suddenly conjure up a caravan of gipsy carts. I
decided to take my father at his word. I picked up my fishing
rod and whistled to Mark. I was now of an age where even my
mother didn't mind my tramping the moors alone but, without
ever having thought out why, I had assumed the countryman's
predilection for having a dog at heel on the mountains. Mark
wasn't a very good sheepdog, but he had the loyalty of his
breed and the courage of an Alsatian.

'Remember to come back in time to milk Hector's cow
before we do the greens!' I heard my father shouting after me.

Now and then as I climbed up the track, I stopped and
looked back, not for any definite reason except that old instinct
tells the man who is used to the mountains to stop before his
breath begins to quicken; that way he can go on for mile after
mile. It was a gentle afternoon, with just enough haze to take
away the horizon and give the Atlantic a feeling of infinity, but
not enough to dim the features of the country, sea, and
moorscape that was widening the higher I went. Not that I
was in much of a mood for noticing anything. I was downcast
but not depressed; depression is a penalty of middle-age. I was
sad that I wouldn't be going to the Northlands school after all,
and yet glad that I would be staying on with Gillespie and my
brother; I was annoyed with myself that I had let my parents
and the teacher down. And I was furious with God. *He* had let
me down. During those months of prayer – first of petition and
then of thanksgiving – I had learnt the truth which I have
heard so many preachers preach since, and that many men
who don't listen to preachers at all find out for themselves in
other ways, that by constant prayer one can establish a
connection with a Power beyond, as real as the closest human
relationship and more fulfilling, and the knowledge of the
existence of a Greater Being. It is a belief that I have never

lost, but a knowledge which I have not always remembered. What I didn't realize that day was that my prayers had been heard all right but that He had just decided to say 'No.'

It isn't difficult to believe, when one's in a place like that, and not in a hurry. I was taking the long way; I was going over the upper shoulder of Bleaval instead of over the hip which would have got me there just the same. And when I got to the top I could see as much as any man can see of the world from one spot. And not just my world alone, but the old world of generations stretching back to forgotten time. Miles down and away to the south-west, the islands of the Sound of Harris (all the ones that the people had seen in new perspective from that first aeroplane) Killegray, Ensay, Shellay and the mysterious island of Pabbay, meaning Priests' Island, still with its ancient ruined chapel standing long after people – far less priests – had been banished from it. On our side of the Sound, on the mainland of Harris itself, Temple Park with its aged temple dating back – according to legend – to Druidic times, but standing upon layer upon layer of older foundations still, showing that man had inhabited that site two thousand years before Christ. The eyes travelled along the white beaches and the empty Atlantic till they reached the standing stone on the fringe of our own new village; a simple standing stone off which nobody would ever have scraped crotal because one would have been defacing the surface of history itself; Steingreidh Stone stood in sight of its replica on Nisabost Point further north, which in turn stood in sight of another of the same on the island of Taransay . . . three simple stones that were links in a whole chain of centres of ancient religious observance, all of them in sight of each other, at one time forming an unbroken chain of vision that included larger centres like the Callernish Stones in Lewis, Brodgar in Orkney and then south again link by link till it reached Stonehenge. Nearer still, from where I sat I could just make out the tip of the spire of St Clement's Church in Rodel (the church out of which that wooden bench at home had come), but although St Clement's is the only cruciform church in the Western Isles its foundations go back long long before the present building – which is only five centuries of age. Long before the modern St

Clement's was built by a Chief of Clan MacLeod in the fifteenth century, there had been a nunnery on the site and it was from there that the island I was going to visit now had derived its mystery and its name.

I had had no thought of visiting Eilean na Caillich when I left home. It was, after all, my father who had put the idea of going fishing into my head. But now that Loch Langabhat with all its wealth of elusive brown trout lay just a short walk down the hill I knew that I wasn't going to bother with the fish, who had so far not bothered with me, but I was certainly going to visit Eilean na Caillich which had been absolutely and firmly forbidden me all my life with no reason given.

In Gaelic the word *cailleach* (of which *caillich* is the possessive case) now means 'old woman' – although my grandparents would have been furious with me if I had used it in that sense, because they were aware of an older meaning still. In ancient times it meant holy woman or nun, and it was from such a person that the island had derived its name although nobody could be sure why. The legend was that, many centuries ago, a nun from the ancient nunnery which preceded St Clement's Church had been wrongly accused and convicted of some heinous sin or other and that she had been banished to the little island on Loch Langabhat for the rest of her days. If it was true it was a cruel banishment because the island is a mere patch in the middle of one of the loneliest lochs in the Hebrides. It isn't so lonely now because a road passes at the far end of it, but in those days of the holy woman's banishment it was in the middle of nowhere and on the uninhabited side of Harris.

Whenever I had asked why I wasn't allowed on to Eilean na Caillich I was just told that it was dangerous, and that was that. But there had always been something which had suggested that I was being fobbed off with a half truth. All I knew about the island, and I had gleaned that accidentally by overhearing somebody mention it, was that there was an underwater causeway to it with a stone that rattled when one stood on it. Now, islands with causeways with warning stones are ten-a-penny throughout the country; usually they were defensive islands, even with fortified castles on them sometimes, and the warning stone was, in effect, an early warning system to give the inhabitants notice of an approaching enemy. But by no stretch of the imagination could Eilean na Caillich be such a place. It was no larger in size than a suburban garden, and part of the punishment for the poor prisoner on it was that she would barely have room to stretch her legs. But why the mystery about it? Why the total ban on our visiting it as children? The subject hadn't arisen for a long time because I had always been in the Northlands during the months of holiday and weather when one might have been most tempted to go stravaiging the moors, and so it would be reasonable to plead – if the need arose – that one had assumed the ban to have lapsed. And what did it matter anyway? I was too big for the fetter rope now. The last time my father had thrashed me I had gritted my teeth and hadn't cried, and as I'd hitched up my trousers with apparent contempt I knew that he was the one who had suffered the greater ignominy and that that form of punishment would never be tried again. I called Mark and set off down the far side of the hill.

It took me longer than I thought to reach the shore of the loch and quite a long time to find the end of the causeway. When I did find it, all the mystery seemed to vanish, and it appeared to be fairly obvious why parents wouldn't want a child on his own tackling the passage. The old stones of the causeway had become worn and rounded with the years – with the wearing of feet in early times maybe, but mostly with the gentle but insistent action of the water, because the wind funnelling down the side of the mountain could raise quite a disturbance in the long narrow loch. And in addition to the wear and tear, the peaty water had caused a slippery slime to form. I knew it would have been dangerous to try the crossing a year or two earlier but now, with more caution and experience and with my rod to use as a balancing pole, I should have no trouble. I set off and soon found it wasn't just as easy as it looked, and I had to abandon all thought of getting across in any kind of dignified way. The only possible way to save myself from a ducking (or worse, since like most islanders I couldn't swim) was to get down to a crouch, balance myself using my rod as a pole in my right hand, and

153

get whatever grip I could with my left hand on the stones of the pathway just under the surface. That way I made slow and steady progress, till suddenly a stone underfoot rocked violently and a crack like a shotgun echoed through the hills. The fright and the lurch nearly landed me in the water, and certainly gave me the fright of my life. But that wasn't all. Was it my imagination? Or was the day darkening over? I felt the beginnings of panic and suddenly realized that I was terribly alone. I looked around and saw Mark standing at the end of the causeway with his tail stiff and the hair of his ruff standing on end. I called to him, but he paid no attention. He put his nose in the air and began to bay; a series of slow eerie whines that echoed back from the rocks. I called him again but he paid no attention. I shouted in anger but he didn't even look my way. Suddenly I felt the beginnings of fear, which is a different thing altogether from fright. I knew that that dog must come with me whether he liked it or not. I felt that unreasonable, uncontrollable feeling of anger against a dumb brute coming over me, that I hadn't experienced since that day I'd been caught hammering the baby rabbit to death because he couldn't live. Forgetting all about danger I plunged back to the shore and grabbed Mark by the neck.

It was madness of course, without rhyme or reason to it. There was nobody to scoff at me for failing to make the crossing; there was nobody to help if I fell in, and I knew that the soggy peaty bottom of the loch could hold one by the ankles. I'd seen sheep's carcasses through the water with their wool and flesh all but gone and their feet still held firm; and I'd seen what had once been a hind.

A dog less loyal than Mark, or worse tempered, would have turned on me and broken away and headed for home. But he didn't. He struggled and protested, but I got him into the water, in which he was normally as happy as a seal; and, using him as a support in my left hand, with my rod still in my right, I started the crazy crossing again. This time I was ready for the warning stone, and when it cracked I didn't even startle. After that the rest of the crossing was quick and required only care. Exhausted, I stumbled on to Eilean na Caillich at last and flopped breathless on the heather. Mark shook himself dry and began to run round the circumference of the tiny island as if he was crazed, barking and baying in turn. I cursed him and threatened him, and at last he lay down as far from me as he could and put his head on his outstretched fore-paws and watched me. I had almost been happier with his noise. As his last whimper died away a total silence came down on the loch and the hills, and the sun stayed behind whichever rain-cloud had obscured it.

After a few minutes my breathing settled down and the strange feeling of eeriness seemed to lift. I began to explore the island, such as it was. At first glance it looked like one of the old rumples of stones peeping through the moorland heather where homes had stood once, except that this particular pile was peeping out of the waters of the loch with one stunted rowan tree growing out of a crevice among the bits of moss and heather.

After I had stood and looked for a few moments, now only feeling a slightly chill curiosity, I could see that there was more shape to the pile of stones than was immediately apparent. As I got used to the contours of them, and was able to eliminate the overgrowing moss and heather from my mind's eye I could make out, quite clearly, the outlines of what had once been the walls of a tiny little cell; I could see where the door had been, and as I went round, on my hands and knees now, I found a long flat stone that had once been a crude lintel. And then my hand went on to a jagged clutch of bones and I choked back a cry and stopped in time and very nearly opted for vomiting instead.

A split second later I was laughing, and the noise of my laughing set the dog whining again till I silenced him. They were bones all right, big bones, but there were feathers among them, and I realized that I was looking down at a heron's nest which I had never seen before close at hand. But instead of my mind being put at ease as I looked, a new apprehension came over me. The nest had two eggs in it, still whole but very very cold and, it didn't require much imagination to conclude, very addled. And I realized that they weren't the bones of one bird but of two, because the skulls and the long beaks were still there. Nor was that all. When I gave up trying to make any sense out of two large dead birds, obviously caught out by death while one was sitting on the nest and one beside it, I noticed another nest with exactly the same set-up. And another just a few yards along. In all a total of 6 herons and, I assume, 6 eggs although they weren't all whole; and all the birds dead. There was no sign of how or why and I just stood silently trying to imagine. And then I heard a voice. Or rather, felt a voice. It came from my ears but at the same time it came from within my head. It said, 'Put off thy shoes from off thy feet for the place whereon thou standest is holy ground.' I felt my knees beginning to give way and my tongue sticking to the roof of my mouth. But I didn't stop to think any more. I yelled 'Mark' and set off rushing over the slippery stones of the causeway, forgetting my rod to support me and making no attempt to cling on to the dog. Not that he waited. This time he gave a yelp and jumped into the water and swam ashore as if he were fetching a stick as he used to do as a puppy. By the time I floundered across, fortunately never having lost foothold completely, he was shaking himself dry and prancing with happiness. I remembered that my rod was still on the island. It was only a simple bamboo rod but even if it had been split cane with a silver reel I wouldn't have gone back for it. Nor would I now.

As I reached the shoulder of the hill I came on the sun again and I convinced myself that it was only the dipping of it into the west in the afternoon that had cast the shadow that had set my imagination going in the first place. But I didn't stop to cast a look behind at Loch Langabhat or Eilean na Caillich, but instead made my way down the mountain, across the moor and home without stopping.

Father was just closing the door of the weaving-shed behind him as I reached the house.

'Were you not able to carry all the fish then? Ach never mind we'll take a creel and I'll go and give you a hand with them after we'd have some food to strengthen us!'

When I didn't respond to the hoary old joke he stopped and looked at me.

'Are you feeling all right?'

'Yes, fine.'

'You don't look it. Where were you?'

'Loch Langabhat.'

He stopped walking and when I looked at him I saw his eyes narrow, but there was no hint of a twinkle in them.

'Did you go on to Eilean na Caillich by any chance?'

'Yes.'

'Well, you had to – some day. I suppose the surest way of making you go was by telling you not to. I'm glad you did, but you were daft to go alone. One slip into that water and you could have been drowned.'

I felt the surprise on my face as I looked at him.

'Have you been?'

'Yes, of course.'

'What happened?'

Now he did smile.

'Come on with you! Every time I tell you a good story you accuse me of making it up. But you're going up to milk Old Hector MacGeachan's cow as usual, aren't you? Why don't you ask him? And you're very pally with George MacLellan. Why don't you tell him that you were on the island and ask him what he feels about it.'

Ever since his sister had died, the village women – and some of the older boys – had taken it in turn to milk old Hector's cow for him. But since the summer holidays had begun the job had devolved more and more on me, just because I was nearer and because I had nothing else to do. So now the morning and evening milking of old Hector's cow was routine. The simple truth, although he would never admit it, was that he was scared of her himself, and one couldn't really blame him because he was getting arthritic and old. One day somebody would tell him to put the cow away and that the villagers would keep him supplied with milk night and morning, but not yet. Although he had no croft of his own the cow represented his independence for Old Hector, and he was glad that the minister who had died had given him a lifetime's grazing rights on the church's land. Which the minister had no right to do because he had no authority to make any promises that could be binding on his successor. But it didn't matter. There had been no successor to the old minister and the Kirk Session had just let Old Hector carry on as before; and when a new minister did come, as was now imminent, it would be unlikely that the Session would allow him retract the old man's only perquisite in life. Just as unlikely as it would be that our village would ever appoint a minister who would be the kind of man who would try.

Although nobody knew it, milking Old Hector's cow was, indirectly, a perquisite for me. The old man had given me his solemn promise that he wouldn't tell anybody that I smoked and so, every night, after I had strained and set the milk for him, I would light up and sit across the fire from him and smoke in comfort instead of crouching behind a dyke out of sight of our own house.

That night I broached the subject of the island after we had both lit up, and immediately I sensed his wariness.

'I wouldn't go near that place if I were you,' he said, 'there's something unchancy about it and there always has been.'

'What happened when you were there?'

'It's not a place I like talking about, especially now that I'm alone in this house.'

That jolted me. The old man obviously felt that whatever he had sensed on Eilean na Caillich could reach out to him in his own house. But that didn't really surprise me. Old Hector belonged to a generation for which the dividing line between superstition and religion was a very narrow one indeed, and very fudged in some areas. I wheedled him, and told him that my father had been on to the island and that it was he who had asked me to speak to him about it. I didn't let slip that I'd been myself because I knew he would question me inside out and that I would end up hearing nothing from him. At last he gave way and told me the story of how he'd been on the island many years before. He'd gone ashore from a rowing boat when he was a ghillie on the loch so he hadn't had to negotiate the causeway, but his story was none the less interesting for that.

When I saw George MacLellan a few days later he was much more forthcoming. George was an extrovert and, now that it was years in the past, he was prepared to laugh the whole thing off as imagination. But he wouldn't go back there again.

The stories the two men told weren't really stories as such at all. Just simple straightforward accounts of the legend of the island and how they had felt an eerie feeling. Neither of them had had anything like the extra gruesome touch of the herons that I'd experienced and still can't explain. What was interesting – and why I wouldn't go back – was that one sentence was common to all the stories. 'Put off thy shoes from off thy feet for the place whereon thou standest is holy ground.'

As I left Old Hector's house on the night that he told me, I remembered that the neighbour immediately next door to us had just got a wireless set, and I called in hoping that they might be listening. They were, and they had company because – instead of destroying social life as radio and television were to do in the years to come – the wireless was an attraction in our village in those days. Very few people had a set, but the few sets there were tended to attract evening visitors to hear what was going on in the world outside, and after the news (listening was carefully rationed because the power was supplied by wet batteries which had to be sent away for re-charge) people tended to sit on and exchange news and conduct village business. The news of the time was of the recruiting of volunteers for the Territorial Army, and it was becoming obvious that the rumours of war had not been so empty after all.

'Sorry to hear you didn't get the bursary,' somebody said, and I was glad it was out in the open. 'Never mind, you'll get another chance next year. In any case if a war starts there won't be much sense in boys going on to High School; they'll just be called up anyway before they're finished.'

'Nonsense,' the man of the house said. 'If there is a war it'll be over in a few months this time, and our boys will be too young to get involved.'

It turned out that two boys from our school had got bursaries – the youngest and the eldest of the candidates. Neither of them belonged to one of the eight families who had set up the new village. Our coterie was still intact, except for two much older girls who had been on the point of leaving before the new village began. And the places vacated by the two successful boys were soon to be filled. Yet another estate on the west coast was being divided into crofts and, till they got a school of their own the children were going to be 'bussed' to us.

Times were, indeed, moving on. The whole of the rich west coast of Harris was now subdivided from being farms into being small-holdings, and the new batch of people coming from the east were really 'returning home' as we ourselves had done, not so long before.

Chapter Fourteen

B Y the time I got back from listening to the men talking about the possibilities of war, mother had gone through to settle the baby and father was alone in the living room.

'Where's Donald?' I asked.

'Where you should be. In bed!'

Gone was the sympathy for my disappointment over the bursary result; gone was the feeling of bond on which we had parted when he had been so mysterious about Eilean na Caillich. I was fairly confident that I hadn't done anything wrong – for the simple reason that I hadn't been in the house – and I racked my brains to think of something that I had done in the recent past that was just redounding on me now. But no. My conscience was relatively clear and, in any case, the fact that Donald was in bed early suggested that it was he who had stirred up some trouble for which everybody else was suffering now.

'Has Donald been doing something wrong?' I asked hopefully.

'Probably. But I haven't discovered it yet.' It was a bad sign when he was being unforthcoming.

'Well, I haven't done anything; I haven't been in.'

'Precisely. Do you remember me asking you to do the greens before you went off gallivanting and nearly getting yourself drowned today? The last thing I said to you before you left was to do the greens when you came back. But I didn't mean when you came back at eleven o'clock at night with the Sabbath only an hour away!'

So that was it! And yet he had given me the get-out himself.

'Well that's all right, isn't it? Nobody's going to play golf on Sunday, and even if somebody does play on Monday it won't be till evening. Hardly anybody plays on Monday.'

'Smart thinking. But not smart enough. Monday's a Bank Holiday and there's a match starting at ten o'clock. That means I've got to be up at five in the morning to get the greens done before they arrive. I'll tell you something; you're going to be up too!'

It was on the tip of my tongue to point out that, after all, he was the one who was being paid to do the greens although I doubted if he could find Number Five without taking them in sequence, but I knew where to draw the line when he was in that kind of mood, and in any case I had more to lose than I had to gain by continuing the argument. I decided to slip off to bed where he couldn't score any fresh points without wakening the baby. The greens had been a source of argument for two years now.

I have always maintained that, away back in the days of Creation, the Almighty, when he had finally remembered to place the Hebrides at all, had intended the undulating swathes of machair land which we had so unimaginatively commandeered for common grazing land, as a golf course. But it took a long time for anybody to cotton on to the Almighty's purpose – a failure of communication which is not altogether peculiar to the Western Isles. But when the revelation came, it came (as the Good Book itself forever stresses) in an unexpected quarter. The doctor, the bank manager, the landlord, the road surveyor, and sundry other members of the leisured classes decided that our Atlantic coast should and would, indeed, be made into a golf course. And the policeman (for all that he was left-handed) concurred. But the *Gentry*, as they deemed themselves, were stymied before the first club was swung; indeed before the first green was made.

While the Articles of Surrender (or whatever they were called) drawn up between the dispossessed landlord and the Board of Agriculture decreed that the former retained the fishing and shooting rights on what had once been his land, in all other respects the jurisdiction over that land now rested with the democratically elected Grazings Committee which represented the crofters. And, while they could not stop the landlord exercising his wild animal and mineral rights, there was not – in that constitution – one fragment of clause which gave anybody the right to march over the common grazing firing hard white balls which could kill a spring lamb or damage an expectant sheep, or, come to that, an expectant mother who might conceivably be milking a cow in the middle of a fairway. So, fired with their newfound enthusiasm, there was nothing the gentry and the policeman could do except come cap in hand to the Grazings Committee to plead their case to a gaggle of horny-handed crofters who knew nothing about golf except that it involved a lot of balls. And, unfortunately, they chose an evening when the crofters were suffering from a dose of bad English. For once, in a manner of speaking, the ball was in their court.

Nowadays everybody in the country knows more about golf than the late Harry Vardon did, for the same reason that even frail old ladies clutching the Queen's telegram can see a snooker developing in the eyes of the man bending over the cue. But it is very difficult to define golf to people who have been conditioned to think all their lives that the highest score wins; it can be obscenely difficult to describe it in a language as capable of ambiguity as English to Gaelic-speaking natives who are accustomed to a language which calls a spade a spade and in which round objects have to be very specifically defined. But, at last, the general idea got through.

And the gentlemen could guarantee that this ball could always be made to travel in a dead straight line?

Well – er – not always, but pretty nearly always.

So there was a danger – just a slight danger – that this hard white ball could wander on to a croft and hit a hen or, Heaven forbid, a child?

The chances were minimal; like winning the football pools.

Like what?

There is a great deal to be said for bi-lingualism, and not least is the legitimate excuse it gives to plead for time to think in one language when one is talking in another. And so the crofters pled for time, which the gentry dreaded as an elastic commodity in the Hebrides; and the men of means began to see their chances of seaside links slipping away. So they tried the last resource of the moneyed classes. Money. Which was what the crofters had been waiting for; but, naturally, they couldn't resolve such a delicate problem haphazardly, however much might be on offer. They didn't want to spoil anybody's pleasure, and it wasn't as if this meant any great loss of amenity; not as if any of the grazing had to be scythed or anything like that.

Well, as a matter of fact, now that somebody had mentioned it there was a small matter of greens. Yes that had nearly been overlooked.

Greens?

Yes. Mown patches round those wee holes that the balls were ultimately going to land in.

But they could be down among the marram grass – the long stiff stuff growing out of the sand where there was no grazing for the sheep anyway.

Well, no. Not quite. It wasn't as easy as that. There had to be a fairly unobstructed run up to the – er – greens somewhere on this side of the marram, so that the marram could be a hazard for any balls which might, very occasionally, fly off course; just as it had been agreed that the crofts would be out of bounds for any balls which, once or twice a year, might go off course in that direction.

It was all becoming clearer now. Ideally the gentlemen wanted those green mown patches at intervals down the middle of the best green grazing. Was that it?

Well, that was one way of putting it.

But of course the greens – these mown patches – they would be very small?

O indeed yes. About – er – ten yards by ten.

About a hundred square yards?

That *was* another way of looking at it, yes.

And how many such patches would there be, very roughly?

That was *one* point there was no 'very roughly' about; there would be exactly nine. And nine things called tees which would be about sixteen square yards, but they wouldn't be mown as often as the greens. The divots usually saw to that.

The what?

Now, under pressure, divots *are* a bit difficult to explain without making them sound like miniature efforts at ploughing, and the gentlemen could not swear that occasional divots might not be uplifted accidentally from sundry other parts of the best grazing as well as from the designated area of the tees. All in all this was beginning to sound like a game with a fair incident of accident. But an accommodation could surely be reached. In all fairness to the gentlemen though, they were overlooking some problems which might be more complicated to solve. For example, if those mown greens had to be so very smooth and flat, would the ever increasing incidence of rabbits (those very productive strong Dutch ones which had been introduced by the landlord himself) be rather a nuisance especially when they started making little practice burrows in the smoothly mown sward?

The landlord squirmed. He was now isolated. Not even his own cronies could be expected to support him when it came to an argument about the advantages of rabbits digging little shallow holes in golfing greens, and so it ended up with him practically pleading with the crofters to trap them, snare them, or ferret them, or do whatever the hell they liked with them. And that, except for the embarrassing business of the money, was all – apart from the matter of the flimsy little wooden bridge which the crofters had, at great cost to themselves, put across the river on the common grazing; but the golfers would be willing to wade (wouldn't they?) because these planks couldn't stand up to constant traffic.

The district surveyor was a forceful man with access to wood and joiners. He was also getting fed up with the whole protracted argument. Yes, he would personally see to it that a solid new arched wooden bridge would be built across the river and would be regarded as a right of way. Now what about a token rental?

A crofter with an astonishingly good head for figures had worked out that nine hundred square yards (including of course those little tees) was not far off a quarter of an acre give or take a few square yards and those divot things, and put that way it sounded quite a lot. But, in view of the generosity of the gentlemen with regard to the bridge and the rabbits, a token rental of fifty-six pounds a year, payable to the Grazings Committee, would seem to be a modest sort of figure.

Fifty-six pounds a year! Good Heavens, that was about the total sum of the rental paid by the total sum of the eight crofters!

Well, well! Put that way, so it was!

And the crofters would be living rent free?

Only in a manner of speaking; the money would go into the coffers of the Grazings Committee. Naturally each crofter would hand over his own rent at term day as usual. But of course, if a score or so of salaried gentlemen were going to find it difficult to raise a pound and a couple of shillings a week between them . . .

Good Lord, there was no question of that. Of course the gentlemen would pay fifty-six pounds a year for the sake of good-will and all the rest of it . . . .

Once the deal had been struck the only other thing that had to be seen to was the appointment of a greenkeeper whose function it would be to keep the nine greens neatly mown, and to keep any little rabbit holes which might appear on the greens from time to time neatly patched up, especially on Saturdays and Bank Holidays which were the only days on which salaried men could admit to being free to play golf – Sunday, of course, being out of the question. The role and salary of greenkeeper were, for reasons which I have never fathomed, allocated to my father, and, in due course the Golfing Committee presented the most unmechanically minded man I have ever known with a complicated petrol motor mower and an instrument for making neat round holes. The latter was to revolutionize the planting of early potatoes.

If my father was unmechanically minded, the boys of the village certainly were not, and if they'd had money they would have paid for the privilege of chuntering along behind a motor machine mowing large square and round patches called greens. We'd have mown the fairways too given a chance, but the Grazings Committee was adamant that that particular chore had to be left to the sheep since the sheepstock was still relatively important, now with the tweed trade improving – even to a crofting community living, technically, rent free.

It was an excellent golf course by any standards, designed, as I have indicated, by the Great Architect Himself. Not one single bunker nor artificial hazard of any kind had to be created. But natural hazards there were in plenty, ranging from wide-mouthed rabbit holes which could no longer be guaranteed not to have gin traps in them, to sand dunes and sand pits and stretches of thick marram grass. To say nothing of the river and sundry little burns. Perhaps the most disconcerting hazard of all was a psychological one in the shape of a tiny knot of eagle-eyed urchins who followed each golfing pair or foursome at a safe distance and in total silence, watching and noting where each golf ball went, but sadly bereft of English when it came to telling. When the last golfer went home, we descended on the course. We kept the best of the recovered balls for ourselves, and, on the following Saturday sold the surplus ones to the most generous payers. We became rapidly addicted to the game. At first we had to make do with heavy walking sticks with the handles shaved to represent club faces, and with odd bits of light iron fencing droppers appropriately shaped. But, over the months, we managed to accumulate a motley set of clubs – usually hickory-shafted ones donated by the younger and friendlier members of the Golf Club; the landlord, in fact, presented a large selection of steel-shafted clubs to the school so that we could play in the intervals. By the time my first attempt at the bursary examination had come round I was playing off scratch even although my style might horrify Niklaus and amuse Trevino.

Occasionally, in the summer and autumn, after I'd received the news of my failure, a flashy car would roll up at our gate and a well dressed tourist in plus-fours would come to enquire from my father, in his capacity as greenkeeper, if he could suggest somebody who might caddy and guide him round the course. The tourist was invariably accompanied by a lady, who was – or purported to be – his wife, whom he was always bent on impressing. His jaw would sag ever so slightly when my father produced me – in ragged trousers and muddy bare feet; in all my years of primary school we never graduated to shoes in summer or to long trousers at all.

These were, I think, the games I enjoyed most in all my golfing life. And the pattern of them was always remarkably the same. We would arrive on the first tee in silence, with the playing couple exchanging little doubtful upper-class glances which, translated in any language meant 'What the hell have we got here?'

Once on the tee I would point out where the first green was – a treacherous one on the lip of a twenty foot deep sandy crater – and I would warn them about the sundry other hazards that lay ahead. The gentleman would always drive off first with great self-confidence; and regardless of whether he hooked, or sliced, or chopped a short one down the middle, he would throw his partner a smug little look which said 'Follow that if you can!' And, of course, she never could – or wouldn't dare.

The light on an Atlantic golf course is very deceptive for someone used to inland courses or east coast links. And golf on an unknown course with unmown fairways is a different ball-game from that on manicured expanses like Turnberry or Lytham St Anne's. I always mentally took my hat off to anybody getting down in under seven on that first green of ours on his first time out; of course I never saw a tourist play a second round. On the second tee I would timidly suggest that it might be quicker if I were allowed to play and indicate the lie of the fairways that way (all for the joy of being able to handle beautifully matched clubs) and the suggestion was always greeted sceptically till, invariably, the lady, if she was of the motherly type at all, would intercede on my behalf. From then on it was fun. I knew every blade of grass on that course, and I had the tremendous psychological advantage that plus-foured gentlemen never expected bare-foot scruffy and ungainly ragamuffins to play golf – far less play well. As the round progressed and I got used to the clubs my confidence would increase, and my opponent's morale would visibly begin to crumble, not only because he was being humiliated in front of his partner (who usually said 'O Charles!' or something to that effect every time he was one down) but because he was being beaten by somebody he was going to have to pay at the end of the round. In all my caddying days I rarely played golf with a good sportsman; in my adult life I played only once with a bad one. And I think the moral has something to do with ragged trousers and bare feet.

But, as that autumn wore on and the ground became waterlogged, my spirits got heavier too as pressure from parents and teacher kept reminding me that I was now on my last chance; it was only by a matter of weeks that I had managed to meet the maximum age requirement that enabled me to have a second attempt at the bursary examination. This time if I failed, my option was quite clear; I would stay on at the village school and then leave to be a crofter or a weaver till such time as I found a job on the mainland. If I wanted a world of books I had eight months in which to ensure a glimpse of it. At the back of my mind I had begun to develop a feeling that though God might be a great designer of golf courses maybe he didn't see them as a guaranteed aid to scholastic success. And although my father had never said 'I told you so' after the shock of the first failure and the way it had come, it did linger in my young memory that on that August Bank Holiday morning – as we mowed the greens together in the dawn – he had said 'Golf's a bit like life you know; it's not getting to the green that really matters – it's how little fiddling about you have to do once you get there. You're on the green now and you've only got a short putt to sink! Remember that and be glad you've got another round to play.'

That was a long time ago. And now May was here again.

Oddly enough I can't remember how or when I went to Leverburgh for the second time. I remember nothing about the examination, except the rules that the teacher had made me learn by heart the day before. I can recite them still. 'Read the paper twice through. Make sure you understand the questions and then read it again. Choose the essay subject you know most about and don't try to write fancy stuff. Leave yourself time to read over what you've written. If you have to make a correction, make it carefully and neatly.'

The memory of Eilean na Caillich had stayed with me over the months and, peculiarly enough, it did something to wipe out the anger that I had felt for having had my prayers ignored. And so I had prayed again as diligently as before, and had found myself struggling hard to push away the thought 'but I'm not leaving it all to You this time'. Perhaps that's what worked.

This time there was no time for rumours. On 8 July I walked out of the village school for the last time as a pupil knowing that I had won, and that I would be going to Tarbert school and the future on 28 August.

On the evening before I left to take up lodgings with Big Grandfather I felt suddenly homesick for a home that I hadn't yet left, and I did what I always did when I wanted to be alone whether for joy or sadness. I walked up the peat road beside the river till I reached the old stone dyke which was the boundary of the croft, as, in the old days it had been the boundary of the big landlords who had held the people in thrall. The stone dyke enclosed, as it still does, the choicest piece of land on the west coast of Harris, known as Scarista Park, but by then the park had been divided between two of the men from the Great War – my father from the army, with a navyman beside him. The river ran down the middle of our croft and then became the boundary between us and the navyman on the left. At the point where I stood and looked back there was a worn step above a gully where my father had placed his feet every second day for nine years with a heavy bag of peat on his back, plodding his way through the kind of life that he had tried to teach me to escape in order that I might live the life he would have chosen for himself. A little further down from me, the river forked before meeting again round what my brother and I had always called 'the big island', where we played at crofts and planted 6 potatoes to represent a field, and a handful of corn to represent a harvest; they had always grown. Then on the river twisted to the spout in the cleft rock at which we filled the water pails; down past the little rectangle of stones with the three legged pot beside it where the white fleeces were dyed crotal to be married with the others in some blend of crotal and white.

Peeping up through a clump of nettles was a cairn of stones that I had forgotten all about; on that August Bank Holiday a year before, while the golf match was in progress, my father in a bout of enthusiasm – or perhaps wanting to take my mind off my failure – had decided that we should begin to collect stones for our new white house. I had laboured with a will for an hour or two and then something had diverted his attention, as had so often happened before. In Scotland cairns are frequently little memorials that people build on mountain tops to prove that they have climbed them; sometimes they're not . . . .

Further down, the river passed the house and the pool where my mother used to rinse out the heavy tweeds when they had been thumped and cleaned and shrunk to the width beyond which they would shrink no more on moorland or on golf course. Then it left us, and passed below the road which hadn't been there when we came to the new village – or at least only the foundations of it had – and as the water reached the machair it widened out into a series of deep pools where we fished for sticklebacks. Two planks used to span it; now the golfers had supplied a beautiful arched bridge of wood which made it more than ever the Tiber of my imaginings from the poem that father had fired my imagination with when I was struggling with English years ago.

With weeping and with laughter
Still is the story told . . . .

Unlike the Tiber, our river never reached the sea. Just after it got down to the white sands it filtered down into them to create patches of dangerous quicksands which one had to get to know, and not only know but try to keep a note of how they changed with excessive floods. You could read them when you got to know them. The quicksands weren't the ridged patches with treacherous looking shallow ditches of water lying between them. No, the quicksands were the peaceful looking flats that caught the light and looked as if one could step on them in perfect safety.

There had been 4 of us when father had built the little temporary house down below me; now we were 6 and the fact that I was moving out and, from now on, would only be coming home for holidays would take a bit of pressure off till father got round to building the new house now that things were getting better. And they were getting better. In 9 years a new village had grown up round the school and the church and the old manse up on the hill. The old manse which had seen the place change from an empty coast to an overcrowded coast, and then swing back to emptiness again, had seen the beginnings of a new village facing a new way of life with new hope. Now here it was, with all the amenities that were modern of their time – an aeroplane landing regularly on its white sands, radio in almost every home, a golf course, and a successful school with a brilliant teacher who could be guaranteed to send at least two pupils out into the world every year. Here was I leaving now – the first boy of the new village. Molly, the first girl, had gone. The trickle was to grow into a steady stream that would grow bigger and bigger, searching for its own bit of sea somewhere. Streams can grow into rivers for sure; they can reach their sea, or like ours sink into the sand. They rarely flow back because that way the hill is against them.